Paula J Campbell

In the

WAITING ROOM

Finding hope and inspiration when facing disappointment

A CIP catalogue record for this book is available from The British Library.

Scripture quotations are taken from:

New International Reader's Version (NIRV). Copyright © 1995, 1996, 1998, 2014 by Biblica, Inc.®. Used by permission. All rights reserved worldwide.

Amplified Bible (AMP). Copyright © 2015 by The Lockman Foundation, La Habra, CA 90631. All rights reserved.

Living Bible (TLB). The Living Bible copyright © 1971 by Tyndale House Foundation. Used by permission of Tyndale House Publishers Inc., Carol Stream, Illinois 60188. All rights reserved.

New Living Translation (NLT). Holy Bible, New Living Translation, copyright © 1996, 2004, 2015 by Tyndale House Foundation. Used by permission of Tyndale House Publishers Inc., Carol Stream, Illinois 60188. All rights reserved.

The Message (MSG). Copyright © 1993, 1994, 1995, 1996, 2000, 2001, 2002 by Eugene H. Peterson.

King James Version (KJV). Public Domain

The Holy Bible, New International Version (NIV) Copyright © 1973, 1978, 1984, 2011 by Biblica, Inc.® Used by permission. All rights reserved worldwide.

New King James Version® (NKJV). Copyright © 1982 by Thomas Nelson. Used by permission. All rights reserved.

ISBN 13 - 978-0-9955725-0-8
Printed in the UK.

THANK YOU

To my loving and supportive family and friends – thank you for all your encouragement along the way.

Thank you to my heavenly Father for the vision and perseverance to see it through.

CONTENTS

INTRODUCTION

As we journey through life, we may be faced with many situations that we find challenging – financial problems, health problems, relational and family issues, work and business problems, to name a few.

One of the issues that I have struggled with is singleness, and there have been times when I've felt down as a result of the impact it has had on my life. I don't believe we were made to go through our whole life alone; we all need support.

Ecclesiastes chapter 4 tells us,

"Two can accomplish more than twice as much as one, for the results can be much better. If one falls, the other pulls him up; but if a man falls when he is alone, he's in trouble. Also, on a cold night, two under the same blanket gain warmth from each other, but how can one be warm alone?

And one standing alone can be attacked and defeated, but two can stand back to back and conquer; three is even better, for a triple braided cord is not easily broken."

(Ecclesiastes 4:9-12, TLB)

Don't get me wrong, I am not advocating having a love triangle! The "triple braided cord" that these verses speak of signifies having God as the third person within a relationship, making it incredibly strong.

This all sounds great, but in reality there are people who

are not married who would love to be.

Some people experience emotional pain and loneliness as a result of this situation, but they often hide it. No one wants to reveal how vulnerable they feel.

Though a great many things have changed in the 21st century, some things have not changed much. When it comes to fundamental human relationships, men and women still want to love and be loved.

My expectation was that I would find someone I loved and wanted to settle down, get married to them and have children. It didn't seem like an impossible dream – it's a pretty normal occurrence on planet earth. So there was no reason for me to think that this experience wouldn't be mine. It has therefore come as a shock to find, as a mature Christian woman, that things haven't quite worked out as I'd planned.

Being surrounded by couples and families in society, and seeing media coverage of celebrity relationships and the Royal family – William, Kate, little George and baby Charlotte – it is sometimes a struggle to be happy and content with being single for so long.

This book, then, is a result of my experience and looks at some of the issues that I've encountered and battled with along the way. We all have our ups and downs and as hard as we may try, sometimes we need a helping hand through those times when we feel down. Maybe a few words of encouragement will help. Knowing that someone else understands how we feel can really make a difference.

In this book I share things that have helped me. During difficult times I have found a great deal of encouragement from the Bible and have explored the experiences of some biblical characters who are real to me. I can identify with the challenges they faced and their heartfelt pain. I am strengthened by the knowledge that they made it through. My hope is that you will find encouragement in this book for your life journey and that you will be able to encourage someone else along the way.

I have included, at the end of each chapter, Bible verses that have encouraged me. I hope they do the same for you. Please choose a verse that you like, read it, meditate on it, and read it at different times throughout the day. If possible, memorise those verses that touch your heart and are relevant to your situation. There is also a section where you can write a prayer to our Heavenly Father, to tell Him how you feel about your situation. God is a good listener who hears and answers prayers. I pray this book will help you to know that He is able to be there for you as you face personal challenges in your life.

Be encouraged,

Paula

Chapter One
IN THE WAITING ROOM

"Lord, how long must I wait? Will you forget me forever?
How long will you turn your face away from me? How
long must I struggle with my thoughts? How long must
my heart be sad day after day?"

(Psalm 13:1-2, NIRV)

How many times in your life have you found yourself stuck in a situation, just waiting? Waiting for something … or someone?

Stuck in a "waiting room".

I remember once sitting in the waiting room of a doctor's surgery – for what seemed like an eternity – waiting for my appointment. It became annoying after a while, because this time round I had actually taken the time to *make* an appointment! I could understand having to wait on the occasions when I'd dropped in as an emergency patient. Then I knew that I was in for a long wait – especially when I saw the trailer-load of people who were also waiting. But I had an appointment, so the least the doctor could do was see me on time! But I had to wait … and wait. Okay, I can wait 5 minutes, but come on, 40 minutes?!

Several things went through my mind during this time.

- **Why me?** *Why am I having to wait instead of being seen on time? What's the point in making an appointment if you are not going to be seen at that time?* I had a sense of entitlement. I had kept my side of this arrangement; I had turned up on time; so I was entitled to be seen on time.

- **It's taking too long!** I knew the doctor was busy, but I had a life to be getting on with. I didn't want to waste my time waiting!
- **What's going on here?** I could see that other people, who had come in after me, were being seen before me! This just wasn't fair. It was unjust!
- **Have I been forgotten?** I wondered if, for some reason, the doctor had overlooked me, somehow deciding that my needs were not as important as those of his other patients.
- **I don't like the way things are done here!** "The way this place is run is rubbish," I thought. "I'm sure I could do a better job of organising things!"
- **I'm fed up with all this waiting!** "Any second now I'm leaving!" I told myself.

Okay, it crossed my mind, but I didn't actually leave. After I had concluded that leaving would only hurt me, and I wouldn't get the help I came for, I sobered up and stuck with it until I got to see the doctor.

I discovered a few things that day.

Firstly, I found out that waiting was not my strong point. Secondly, I realised that getting upset about it didn't change one single thing and it definitely didn't make the time go any quicker. Lastly, I knew I needed to learn patience, and how to wait with a better attitude.

As I recall, to alleviate my concerns I'd asked the receptionist if I had been forgotten. She assured me that I had not been – that it had been a very busy surgery that day and I would definitely be seen. After that, instead of moaning some more, I'd decided to read a magazine to take my mind off the wait.

In retrospect, I realise I should have done that in the first place. It would have helped me to turn my attention to something else; to remain positive instead of focusing on the negative. Partly to blame was my expectations: I had an appointment; I didn't expect to have to wait. Therefore I wasn't prepared for the unexpected delay and my attitude reflected that. On reflection, I could have used the time to read my Bible, or an inspiring book. I could have played a game, done a crossword, prayed for my family and friends, prayed for other patients who were ill, prayed for the doctors, prayed for more patience! I could have waited differently.

You'll see that the subject of waiting is close to my heart. When it comes to relationships, I have been in the "Singles Waiting Room" for years! Decades! In fact, I'm still waiting…

At first it wasn't a problem. I was too busy to be bothered. I dated, was in relationships at times, and assumed that when I had finished all the things I wanted to do – achieving an education, establishing a good career, managing my life well, etc – that finding a husband would naturally happen. I would get married. I would have children, like generations of people have done before me, since Adam and Eve.

Well, wasn't I in for a shock when that didn't happen! I felt as though I was in a waiting room and had been forgotten.

Fear and panic set in. Not at first, but in my mid-thirties. As the years went by it became harder to remain positive. I became depressed.

We all go through ups and downs in life, but at times situations persist which seem to bombard us on what appears to be a constant basis. Sometimes our "downs" continue and we find we are not able to bounce back as quickly as before. On-going stress and feelings of being overwhelmed can lead to depression – a dark lonely place where there seems to be no end, no solution, no light at the end of the tunnel.

This is the place I reached with my singleness. I lost hope and fell into despair. I felt as though I had tumbled to the bottom of a deep, dark pit and could not climb my way out. I was so exhausted trying to deal with all the problems I faced that my head hurt. At times I was in such despair and emotional pain that my chest and stomach hurt as well as my head. Sometimes I cried inconsolably.

My grandmother used to sing a well known spiritual:

Nobody knows the trouble I see,
Nobody knows but Jesus. Nobody knows the trouble I see
Glory hallelujah!
Sometimes I'm up, sometimes I'm down
Oh, yes, Lord
Sometimes I'm almost to the ground
Oh, yes, Lord

These words encapsulate the way I still feel at times, but over many years I have learnt to share my sorrows and pain with my heavenly Father in a Journal. He has been my therapist – the One I can confide in – and His Word has been the therapy to heal my broken spirit and emotions.

This is an extract from one of my journals:

Sunday 2nd December 2012
"'Even now' declares the Lord. 'Return to me with all your heart, with fasting and weeping and mourning. Rend your heart and not your garments; return to the Lord your God. For He is gracious and compassionate, slow to anger and abounding in love, and He relents from sending calamity. Who knows? He may turn and have pity and leave behind a blessing.'"

(Joel 2:12-14, NIV 1982 Ed.)

Father, my feelings of sadness are overwhelming. As I read what I wrote over a year ago, I think, what has changed for me on an emotional level in this area of my life? It is still a thorn in my flesh. A relationship, or the lack of one, still has the power to devastate me and break me.

I feel so vulnerable inside that I can't cope with life itself. Last night, last week, two Sundays ago, I was an emotional wreck … lonely, crying, so low, distressed and in pain. I don't really understand why this is so deeply entwined with everything in my life. It totally affects how I feel, how I view my life.

I feel as though being without a husband is a measure of who I am, so no husband means I am nothing. No one wants me, so I must not be valuable or special … which must mean I don't even value myself, either?!

That's how it seems anyway.

The pain feels unbearable and never ending. I try so hard to rise up from this, to be hopeful and believe, but Father, I just find myself sinking under the heaviness of the pain. Please forgive me, Father, for my distrust of you – for not believing that you can do "All things" for me. It's not that I don't believe you can do it, because I've seen you provide husbands for many of my friends, but I'm still waiting, and have been for such a long time – as if you have forgotten me. Yet I know you have not forgotten me! In so many ways you have shown yourself to be so very close to me, hearing and answering my call for help. In the past year you have done amazing things for me! So Father, I know you love me and you do answer my prayers in big ways and small ways. Please help me not to lose hope, and to trust you to provide the husband who is right for me, at the right time. I love you always.

* * *

Singleness had been a good thing, but now it was no longer fun. It seemed as though everyone around me was getting married and having kids. I didn't feel that there were many people who could understand or relate to my situation as an older single woman. I think some people assumed that because I was older, I could cope with being single, or that I didn't want to get married!

I talked to God about the specific issues I was facing and how I was feeling. I also opened up about how I felt to a couple of my single female friends. I realised they shared many of the frustrations and pains that I was experiencing! We were all affected in different ways, but somehow we never let it show. We held our hurt inside and out of sight.

How many reading this are walking around hurting for one reason or another, afraid to show it?

For me, it helped to know that I was not alone … and not crazy. (Okay, maybe some people think I'm a little crazy).

I'm still single and at times I feel low. As a way of dealing with my situation during my dark times, I try to remember times when God has come through for me in the past – when He has provided solutions and helped me to rise above the difficulties. I remember the good times.

I pray and read Bible promises to encourage myself. I read them over and over again to remind myself that God loves me and will be there for me. That He *is* there with me.

I try to fill my spirit with hope. I try to fight the despair. It is an on-going battle that I have to consciously fight and not give up. Some days are better than others, but it is my desire to live the abundant life that Jesus came to give me, and I have an opportunity each day to strive towards that goal.

"I am come that they might have life, and that they might have it more abundantly."

(John 10:10, KJV)

I'm often confronted with the thought that as a Christian I shouldn't get depressed. Where is my faith? It's as though my faith and trust in God have evaporated. But I acknowledge that I'm human and frail.

We all have burdens that we find hard to bear and each person deals with them differently. We are not all the same and we need to recognise that. Just as we are built differently as men and women, and as individuals we have varying physiques – some tall, some short, slim, large, muscular, fast, and slow – so we are wired differently when it comes to our emotions. What is easy for one person to deal with will crush another. Understanding this should help us to be more compassionate and caring towards one another – to *"Carry each other's burdens"* (Galatians 6:2).

We are also blessed to have a loving God, who understands our weakness and calls us to give Him our burdens so that He can give us rest.

"Come to me, all you who are weary and burdened, and I will give you rest. Take my yoke upon you and learn from me, for I am gentle and humble in heart, and you will find rest for your souls. For my yoke is easy and my burden is light."

(Matthew 11:28-30)

We read in the Bible that even a strong prophet like Elijah faced his times of depression. 1 Kings 19:3-6 tells us that Elijah was afraid that Jezebel would kill him.

"Elijah was afraid and ran for his life … he … went a day's journey into the desert. He came to a broom tree, sat down under it and prayed that he might die. 'I have had enough Lord,' he said. 'Take my life; I am no better than my ancestors.' Then he lay down under the tree and fell asleep. All at once an angel touched him and said 'Get up and eat.' He looked around, and there by his head was a cake of bread baked over hot coals and a jar of water. He ate and drank and then lay down again."

When Elijah was in the depths of depression God sent an angel to look after him. I believe the Bible records the distress and problems of various characters so that we can identify with them and not feel alone as we battle with our own difficulties – whatever they may be. We find encouragement in knowing that God was there for them. Therefore, He will not leave us alone and helpless now.

Reflect:
If you ever feel that God has forgotten about your needs, just remember that He made you and He loves you too much to ever forget you.

Meditate:
"Can a mother forget her child and not have love for her own son? Yet even if that should be, I will not forget you."

(Isaiah 49:15, Living Bible TLB)

"Pay attention ... for you are my servant; I made you, and I will not forget to help you."

(Isaiah 44:21)

"I will delight in them and not forget them."

(Psalm 119:16)

"For the Lord your God is merciful – He will not abandon you nor destroy you nor forget the promises He has made..."

(Deuteronomy 4:31)

Pray:

Write a prayer to your heavenly Father and tell Him how you feel. Also tell Him what you need.

Chapter Two
DESIRE OF THE HEART

"The Lord God said, 'It is not good for the man to be alone. I will make a helper suitable for him.'"

(Genesis 2:18)

Everywhere we go we are bombarded with messages – images, films, TV, books, magazines, music videos, posters, billboards – all kinds of media that either promote or depict relationships. Companies sell their merchandise by giving the impression that wearing their perfume, aftershave, clothes, footwear, drinking their brand of alcohol, or driving a certain type of car, will make us more attractive and relationship-worthy. It seems as though the most important thing in the world is to be in a relationship – and there is a good reason for this.

Throughout the Bible we read about many relationships and marriages. Whether good or bad, all the details are there. Marriage was a foundation pillar of God's creation from the very beginning of time. In Genesis, when God created Adam and Eve, we see that,

"God created man in his own image ... Male and female he created them..." and *"God blessed them."*

(Genesis 1:27, 28)

It was God who said, *"It is not good for man to be alone..."* ...and made a woman suitable for man as a helper (Genesis 2:18).

To show the closeness of the relationship between a husband and wife God made the woman from a rib of the man, so that they would be a part of each other, treasure each other, and care for each other in a special way. Acknowledging this, Adam said,

"This is now bone of my bones and flesh of my flesh."

(Genesis 2:23, KJV)

In the New Testament, Paul writes in Ephesians 5:25, 28, 33,

"Husbands, love your wives just as Christ loved the church and gave himself up for her… in this same way husbands ought to love their wives as their own bodies. He who loves his wife loves himself … Each one of you also must love his wife as he loves himself, and the wife must respect her husband."

The love, respect, closeness, unity, help and oneness that characterises the marriage relationship was meant to be, from the very beginning of creation. God made a woman suitable for man. A woman was specially designed to be part of this loving relationship. The two would become *one*.

"For this reason a man will leave his father and mother and be united to his wife, and the two will become one flesh."

(Ephesians 5:31)

Considering all of this, I do not believe that I am misguided in asking God for a husband and hoping to receive one. I was not made to remain alone. I was created to be a part of a special, intimate relationship.

Our desire for companionship, expressed through marriage,

is to be acknowledged as a basic human need. It is a vital component of our design. It's the way we were made by God.

I accept that there are those who have the "gift" of being single. For them, singleness is absolutely right, and I don't devalue them for a moment. But I do believe that the ability to remain single all your life *is* a *special* gift. It is not something that everyone is able to do.

The apostle Paul stayed single his whole life and said, *"I wish that all men were as I am..."* He said this because he had in mind his ability to focus single-mindedly on spreading the Gospel. But immediately he acknowledged;

"...But each man has his own gift from God, one has this gift, another has that ... It is good for them to stay unmarried, as I am. But if they cannot control themselves, they should marry, for it is better to marry than to burn with passion."

(1 Corinthians 7:7-9)

My understanding is that God has made us with desires for companionship, intimacy, passion and sex. He does not expect us to stay single if we do not have that gift. He knows that we may find it difficult to keep our feelings under control.

I have sometimes heard people say that I shouldn't feel lonely, or be concerned about getting married when I have a relationship with God, because God is all I really need. I do not believe that desiring marriage devalues my relationship with God or takes anything away from my need to have a relationship with my Creator.

God is our Father and He made us to have an intimate relationship with Him, as well as desiring companionship from another human being. God made us with that need. He acknowledged it by providing for its fulfilment in marriage. He also wanted to continue His relationship and communication with us as individuals. He walked and talked with Adam and Eve in the Garden of Eden (Genesis 3:8-10). Even after mankind sinned, He still walked with Enoch (Genesis 5:24). God has always maintained a dialogue with us through His Word.

"'Come now, let us reason together' says the Lord, 'Though your sins are like scarlet, they shall be as white as snow.'"

(Isaiah 1:18, NKJV)

God loves us and wants a close relationship with us. Jesus was willing to die for us to show the depth of the Father's love for us. God Himself points to marriage as a picture of the deep, intimate love He has for us:

"Husbands love your wives ... as Christ loved the church and gave himself up for her."

(Ephesians 5:25)

The Bible illustrates a love that is giving and not selfish. This unselfish love is reciprocal – given and received by a man and a woman, so that both experience love together and have their needs met.

God's love is big enough for us to love Him and love our spouse.

As a young woman I imagined that one day I would be married. I was never interested in having a big wedding with lots of fuss. I had attended many weddings and helped at many more. There was so much focus on "the Big day" that I wondered sometimes if enough thought had been given to the marriage that would follow. Over time, sadly some of those marriages have not lasted. I am often shocked and disappointed when I hear about a marriage break-up within my family or friends. Why couldn't they work out their issues? What happened to their marriage vows? Did they not believe, "For richer, for poorer… 'til death do us part"?

It seems that for some, staying together forever was impossible after all. Despite their good intentions and all the good times, it's as though the love, the hopes and dreams, and the happiness they shared at the beginning no longer existed at the end.

I ask myself, *will the same thing happen to me?* Do I allow my hope for having a good marriage one day to die, as it has for those who have parted acrimoniously? Do I choose to believe that God will *not* bless me with a husband? Or do I believe that God is able to provide for my need, just as He provided Eve to meet Adam's need?

I choose to have hope and believe God *can* and *will* give me the desire of my heart.

Until such time, I remain occupied. I work and use my talents and abilities to do all the good I can. I think I understand why Paul wished that everyone was single like him. We have more opportunity to devote our time to do God's work, help those in need and spread the gospel, (1 Corinthians 7:32-35). When a person has a spouse and children they have many other responsibilities that shouldn't be neglected, therefore they have less time available for God's business.

That said, however, when parents raise their children to know God in a happy home, and have a loving, strong relationship with their spouse, they are a great example of God's love in this world. The gospel is preached without words. What a wonderful object lesson.

Whether single or married, we can be devoted to God. If it is your desire to be married, continue to talk to God about it. He wants to be a part of your life and is interested in your heart's desire. Let us trust God to fulfil His promises.

"May He give you the desire of your heart and make all your plans succeed."

(Psalm 20:4)

"Delight yourself in the Lord and He will give you the desire of your heart."

(Psalm 37:4)

Reflect:

God knows what you desire. Put Him first and trust Him to work things out for your best.

Meditate:

"The Lord will guide you always; He will satisfy your needs in a sun-scorched land and will strengthen your frame. You will be like a well-watered garden, like a spring whose waters never fail."

(Isaiah 58:11)

"For the Lord God is a sun and shield; the Lord bestows favour and honour; no good thing does He withhold from those whose walk is blameless."

(Psalm 84:11)

Pray:

Write a prayer to your Heavenly Father and tell Him how you feel. Tell Him the desires of your heart:

Chapter Three
SELF-ESTEEM AND OTHER ISSUES

"Now Laban had two daughters, the name of the older was Leah and the name of the younger was Rachel. Leah had weak eyes, but Rachel was lovely in form and beautiful."

(Genesis 29:16-17)

I find the story of Leah and Rachel an interesting one. You can read it in Genesis chapters 29 and 30. Jacob had travelled to his mother Rebecca's country in order to escape the anger of his brother Esau, whom he had wronged. On his arrival he was blessed to meet a beautiful girl called Rachel at a well.

Possibly it was the same well where his mother, Rebecca, had met the trusted servant of his grandfather, Abraham. The servant was on a special mission to find a wife for his master's son, Isaac – Jacobs's father. Rebecca later became the bride of Isaac. It's funny how God works things out.

Jacob was introduced to Rachel's father, Laban, and welcomed into their home. He was, after all, family – Laban's nephew. After a month of working for Laban, Jacob agreed to work for a further 7 years in order to gain the hand in marriage of his younger daughter, Rachel. Jacob loved Rachel so much that all those years of working only seemed like a few days to him (Genesis 29:20).

Jacob was so happy to eventually marry his bride, but on the morning after the night before he got a terrible shock. He discovered that he'd been stitched up and was now married to "weak eyed" Leah – Laban's older daughter – instead of the "beautiful" Rachel!

I just love the way the Bible says it:

"When morning came, there was Leah! So Jacob said to Laban, 'What is this you have done to me? I served you for Rachel, didn't I? Why have you deceived me?"

(Genesis 29:25)

What a shock! What a deception!

What irony! A deceiver deceived by a deceiver!

Jacob shouldn't have been surprised. He was no stranger to deception himself. He had deceived his own father into giving him his brother Esau's birth right. But that's another story (see Genesis 27).

Apart from Laban deceiving Jacob, could Leah also have been complicit in this plan? Maybe Leah and Rachel had no choice in the matter because their father had forced them into this arrangement for his own greed? He would benefit from Jacob's free labour for another seven years in order to marry Rachel.

Who knows? The Bible doesn't really say. But I wonder what was going on for Leah. I think the fact that the Bible plainly says that Rachel was "lovely in form and beautiful" but does not give a similar glowing description of Leah is significant. The phrase that says she had "weak eyes" seems to suggest she was not beautiful, and her father didn't think anyone would want to marry her, hence he deceived Jacob into marrying Leah.

If Leah didn't already have a self-esteem issue, then this incident must have given her a major one! How could a father force his daughter into a loveless marriage, knowingly subjecting her to a life of misery?

It is possible that Rachel was her father's favourite; that Leah, feeling unloved by her father, was hoping that through marriage she would finally have someone to love her. How painful to have her hopes dashed, again.

Parents play a huge role in a child's upbringing. What they say and do, and how they treat their children, contributes to the process of moulding a child's character, self-esteem and confidence.

Fathers play a vital role in helping their daughters to feel valued and secure in their love. I believe this lays a healthy foundation for the way a woman will view herself in the future. To not feel valued or loved by your father can deeply affect how you feel about yourself. It can lead to an emptiness inside; to a sense of never feeling good enough; feelings of rejection; to be always seeking love, sometimes in the wrong places; it can lead to bad relationship choices. Each time things don't work out, our self-esteem is eroded even more.

But no matter what kind of less-than-perfect "Laban-like" father we have had, we can be sure that our Father God is not like that. He is compassionate and loving and His love is unshakable.

"Though the mountains be shaken and the hills be removed, yet my unfailing love for you will not be shaken... says the Lord, who has compassion on you."

(Isaiah 54:10)

In Jacob's culture, traditionally it was the eldest daughter who should be married first. Yet here was Leah's younger sister, about to get married ahead of her, leaving her unmarried. I don't think this would have helped her confidence and self-esteem. Here was an eligible bachelor who had no interest in her, but lavished love, attention and devotion on her younger sister for 7 years. She probably felt very unattractive since she was unable to find a husband. Her plain looks were always overshadowed by the beautiful Rachel.

I'm sure Leah is not unique in having "weak eyes" (whatever that may be, let's call it "issues"). We all have issues – those "weak" areas in our lives, the things that make us feel vulnerable. It might be a scar we wished we didn't have, or our height, or weight, or shape, or hair, or nose or tummy or other features … The list goes on. Whatever it is, we have this tender spot that hurts when people make a comment about it because it's something we don't like about ourselves.

How often do we compare ourselves, or feel compared, to other women (or compared to other men, it you're a man)? It is probably women we know, just as much as the stars, models and celebrities we see in the media. We are all unique, special individuals, made by God, yet in some way we want to be like somebody else.

Maybe Leah wanted to be like Rachel, to have what Rachel had. After all, it appeared that beauty had its benefits. Rachel was getting a husband!

But to conclude that the only way she could get a husband was through deception must have been the final humiliation.

How awful to feel invisible, overlooked and rejected. How painful not to receive the love you desire. It is quite possible that Leah was genuinely in love with Jacob and hoped that he would grow to love her back over time if they were married. But to deceive him into marriage? How could Leah not see that this would go badly for her? Maybe that was her weakness: she couldn't see that far ahead. It is also possible that the other option she faced seemed a worse fate: to carry the stigma of being single for the rest of her life; to be alone, without a husband, without children. It may have been too much to bear.

How often, as single people, are we tempted to enter into unsuitable relationships? We know that we know better – a trusted friend may have told us as much – and we know that if we were in our "right minds" we wouldn't consider it. But, for some strange reason, we go ahead with it. Maybe it's because we feel vulnerable, lonely, in need of attention, affection, TLC, sex… We might even think that somehow, in our delusion, there is a chance that it could work out.

The truth is, at times we are not always as strong as we'd like to be, or as honest with ourselves as we should be. Sometimes we are weak. Our eyes are weak. Like Leah we don't see clearly. But if we continue down that path, like Leah, we are heading for a life of misery.

Can you imagine if, after the first week of marriage, your husband went off with another woman – and it turned out to be your younger sister!? Worse still, he loves her and not you. How could anyone live with that pain? Poor Leah.

And yet … I am always amazed by God's mercy. When our lives are in a mess, He still loves us. He still helps us, even when we are the ones who have made the mess. The Bible tells us that,

"When the Lord saw that Leah was not loved, he opened her womb, but Rachel was barren."

(Genesis 29:31)

What a turn around! Leah was being compensated for not being loved. God gave her the children she wanted. She was receiving blessings. She had four sons, one after the other: Reuben, Simeon, Levi and Judah. The meaning of Leah's sons' names provide a clear insight into how she was feeling, revealing her misery in a loveless marriage:

"She named him Reuben (He has seen my misery), for she said 'It is because the Lord has seen my misery. Surely my husband will love me now."

(Genesis 29:32)

What desperation! Leah hoped that by having children her husband will love her. Feeling unloved she continued to pray to God that her situation would change.

"'Because the Lord heard that I am not loved, he gave me this one too.' So she named him Simeon (one who hears)."

(Genesis 29:33)

But having another baby didn't work. Jacob still didn't love her.

Have you ever stayed in a relationship because you hoped to receive the love you needed, but you didn't, and yet you still remained? I believe that a lack of self-esteem and of self-worth often makes us accept what is unacceptable. At times we may feel trapped in a toxic relationship, but to leave or stay seem equally uninviting. Then it becomes a case of "better the devil you know". At other times it may be a sense of resignation: "Well, I made my bed, now I have to lie in it. It's my fault, so I'll have to live with this." I can imagine Leah saying something similar to herself: "Surely things are not *that* hopeless? They could change."

Genesis 29:34 says,

"Again she conceived and when she gave birth to a son she said, 'Now at last my husband will become attached to me, because I have borne him three sons.' This child she named Levi (which means attached)."

Leah persisted with the same method that wasn't working. She hoped that by providing him with children Jacob would become attached to her, bonded to her – but it wasn't happening. No matter how much she prayed there was no change in their relationship. She had a husband, but not his love. She had his children, but not a bond with him.

I'm not sure I could live with that. Who would want to? Can you make someone love you? I doubt it. Leah couldn't.

To be loved and to give love is essential in any happy relationship. Things cannot be one-sided – both parties have to give and receive love.

Having children without the love of her husband was never going to be a pleasant experience for Leah. We can see her pain and I'm sure it did not help her self-esteem. Yet, somehow she lived with it. I would not want to be in her shoes, but it is not good for us to cast judgement when people settle for less than the ideal. We may not understand it, but it's the life they have chosen.

As a single woman who wants to be married, to be attached, there are times when life can be miserable. You hope to meet that special man, yet nothing changes. You hope that a relationship you're having will work out, but then it ends. These things can reinforce the negative feelings we have about ourselves.

"There is something wrong with me…"

"I'm not beautiful like X…"

"I haven't got a figure like those models on the catwalk…"

"I'm not young and men only want young women…"

"Men don't even look at me…"

At times, negative thoughts and feelings like these have caused me to despair, leading to a deep depression. The pain and distress is unimaginable. It seems unending, as though nothing will ever change.

And yet … I believe change is possible.

Something happened in Leah. The next time she conceived, something was different.

"She conceived again and when she gave birth to a son she said, 'This time I will praise the Lord' so she named him Judah (which means praise). Then she stopped having children."

(Genesis 29:35)

Leah desperately wanted something that she just couldn't have. No matter how hard she tried, nothing worked; her husband just didn't love her. But she did have God's love and He was giving her children to demonstrate His love. Leah, though unloved by her husband, was given the honour of giving birth to Levi, whose descendants would be favoured as the priests in God's holy sanctuary. Also, it would be through Judah's line that King David and Jesus, the Saviour of the world, would come. Maybe Leah had finally seen what her weak eyes couldn't see before – that she was being given wonderful blessings to praise God for, so she needed to express that appreciation to the Lord.

When we are suffering, it is difficult to praise God. It may have taken years, but Leah eventually made a decision to praise the Lord for His blessings, rather than focusing on her misery. Only God can really help us to do this. When we have a thankful heart and appreciate the things that He is constantly providing for us, it can help to lift our spirits. Praising God brings joy to the soul.

"The joy of the Lord is your strength."

(Nehemiah 8:10)

Please help us to show our gratitude to you more, Father, and help us to praise you. Even when things are not as we would like them to be, help us to praise you anyway. There is always something in our life that we can thank you for – please help us to find it and thank you for it. For the blessing of life and breath itself, let us have a thankful heart and, like Leah, say, "Praise the Lord."

Reflect:

You are a wonderful, loved child whose Father is the King of the Universe. That is definitely something to be happy about.

Meditate:

"I will be a Father to you and you will be my sons and daughters, says the Lord Almighty."

(2 Corinthians 6:18)

"The Lord appeared to us in the past, saying: 'I have loved you with an everlasting love; I have drawn you with loving-kindness.'"

(Jeremiah 31:3)

"Because the Sovereign Lord helps me, I will not be disgraced. Therefore have I set my face like flint, and I know I will not be put to shame."

(Isaiah 50:7)

"I praise you because I am fearfully and wonderfully made."

(Psalm 139:14)

"...I am like an olive tree flourishing in the house of God; I trust in God's unfailing love for ever and ever. I will praise you for ever for what you have done; in your name I will hope, for your name is good."

(Psalm 52:8-9)

Pray:
Write a prayer to your Heavenly Father and tell Him how you feel. Tell him about any issues you have that you need His help with:

Chapter Four
WHO REALLY HAS IT ALL?

"And when Rachel saw that she bare Jacob no children,
Rachel envied her sister and said unto Jacob,
'Give me children or else I die.'"

(Genesis 30:1)

Sometimes we look at other people's lives and, from the outside, it appears that they have it all. So many things seem to be going right for them. Maybe they have a wonderful job, a great home, a nice car, good health, a husband and family … everything seems fantastic and happy in their life. But we do not always know the inside story; what's really going on. *Do they really have it all?*

Initially, when I read the story of Rachel and Jacob I thought, "Ahh, what a fabulous love story!" But their story has such a twist. Despite the fact that Rachel was beautiful (Genesis 29:17), loved and married (Genesis 29:30), things were not exactly ideal for her.

First, her older sister, Leah, got in the way by marrying Rachel's intended husband first. Three in a marriage is not great. But eventually things got much WORSE – there ended up being four women to one man in the marriage (as we will discuss later)! Isn't that just too much? Especially if you had planned for it to be just you and your husband. You can read about the drama in Genesis chapters 29 and 30.

Second, as if things weren't difficult enough for Rachel, having to share her husband with her sister, then Leah had four sons with Jacob, one after the other! When Rachel found out that she couldn't have children herself, that must have been very hard to bear. Genesis 30:1 says,

"And when Rachel saw that she bare Jacob no children, Rachel envied her sister and said unto Jacob, 'Give me children or else I die.'"

Rachel was obviously unhappy. She was so unhappy at being childless that even the love of her husband couldn't console her. Imagine: having no children left her feeling so bad that she wanted to die.

Why did she feel like this? Maybe it was the pain and stigma of being barren, feeling unfulfilled; thinking that her hopes and dreams of having a family would never be realised; feeling that her life was not blessed. I don't know if other women who've not given birth ever feel like this, but sometimes I feel as though I am an unfulfilled woman. As a woman I'm specially created to "be fruitful and multiply". My body was designed with the ability to procreate; my monthly menstrual cycle reminds me of this, but goes by failing to achieve its ultimate goal.

There have been times when I've walked down the high street, seen pregnant women or mum's with babies, and felt sad and upset. There was a sinking feeling in my stomach as I considered that this experience, this blessing of carrying a baby in my womb, may never be a part of my life. I felt a sense of grief; a sense of loss.

Having a baby is such an amazing thing. It's a miracle when babies are born! But being a parent is not easy. Each stage of a child's development carries its own issues. At the same time, it can be such a challenge to handle the emotions and practical difficulties of having a baby, or child, with health problems or special needs of any kind.

It is understandable that we may, like Rachel, feel envious of others who have husbands and children. We probably also feel bad whenever this emotion wells up in us. It is not easy to see others being blessed over and over again when our situation remains the same – and to still remain gracious. We don't always handle this too well.

Poor Rachel, I can understand her heartfelt pain. Her sister has given birth to four children and she hasn't had one. Her emotions were so intense that she began to think irrationally: *"Give me children or else I die!"*

Obviously Jacob didn't have a problem producing babies, so it wasn't him who was causing her barrenness. So why was she saying this?

Rachel had to blame someone and he was getting it! No wonder Jacob was angry with her and told her to face the truth, because such matters are in God's hands.

"And Jacob's anger was kindled against Rachel; and he said 'Am I in God's stead, who hath withheld from thee the fruit of the womb?'"

(Genesis 30:2)

Sometimes when the thing we want isn't happening we get upset with others, or even ourselves, when maybe we are afraid to admit we are upset with God. But how can we tell anyone that – much less say it to God Himself? And yet, we need to be honest with ourselves and God.

It is likely that Rachel knew it was pointless to blame Jacob for making her barren, but she was not happy with the current situation and this was her way of expressing her pain. But then Rachel decided to come up with her own plan of action to change things. She gave her maidservant Bilhah to Jacob as his wife, so that her maid would bear children for her in a type of surrogacy. Talk about complicated! But isn't that typical of us as human beings? We complicate things when we don't wait on God.

Through Bilhah, Rachel was able to have Dan and Naphtali. But this only caused more complications. Because Leah had stopped having children herself, she then decided to do the same thing as Rachel, having further children through her own maidservant, Zilpah.

Zilpah bore Gad and Asher for Leah. What a carry on! This started as a love story, but turned into a wrestling match between two sisters.

"And Rachel said, with great wrestling's have I wrestled with my sister and I have prevailed."

(Genesis 30:8)

Somehow this episode brings back memories of Jacob and Esau. From the very beginning, when Rebekah was pregnant with them, they were fighting:

"...and the children struggled together within her"

(Genesis 25:22)

Yet again there is struggle and wrestling in Jacob's relationships.

Relationships can be a struggle, even our relationship with God. At times we struggle to understand what He is saying to us, or why He allows certain problems to exist in our lives, especially when things could be so much easier. Why must our lives be so hard? Isn't He there to make our burdens light? The truth is, God does not do things in the way we expect or think. He allows us to go through difficulties, but He is always there to hear us when we call to Him for help, and He will support us through the challenges we face.

Like Rachel, we may feel forgotten by God and try to work out our own plan, but instead, if we continue to have faith and call on Him, He will answer and work things out according to His will and in His own time.

Romans 8:28 says, *"All things work together for good..."*

"And God remembered Rachel, and God hearkened to her, and opened her womb. She said 'God hath taken away my reproach.'"

(Genesis 30:22-23)

Eventually, Rachel was blessed with two sons: Joseph, and later on, Benjamin. God used Joseph to become a strong, compassionate leader who was able to save his people and the nation of Egypt in a time of famine. The first King of Israel, Saul, came from the tribe of Benjamin.

God does hear! Even though sometimes it appears that He will never answer. Often we cannot understand His thinking or His way of doing things, but we need to trust Him through the situation.

God has His own way of blessing us with special blessings. We should never underestimate His love for us. To feel heard by God and have our prayers answered brings such joy, so we need to keep hopeful and hold onto His promises.

"Yet the Lord longs to be gracious to you; therefore He will rise up to show you compassion. For the Lord is a God of justice. Blessed are all who wait for Him!"

(Isaiah 30:18)

Rachel felt that her disgrace had been taken away. God is able to take away whatever pain, scars and stigma we may have. He can heal us and will remember us in our distress. He can turn our sorrow and mourning into joy.

"Then young women will dance and be glad, young men and

old as well. *I will turn their mourning into gladness; I will give them comfort and joy instead of sorrow."*

(Jeremiah 31:13)

Reflect:
In life you will experience tough times, but there is always hope for a brighter future.

Meditate:
"You will surely forget your trouble, recalling it only as waters gone by. Life will be brighter than noonday, and darkness will become like morning. You will be secure, because there is hope."

(Job 11:16-18)

"Though he slay me, yet will I hope in Him ... Indeed, this will turn out for my deliverance."

(Job 13:15-16)

Pray:
Write a prayer to your Heavenly Father and tell Him how you feel. Ask Him to fulfil His promise of hope in your life:

Chapter Five
JUST ASK

"Ask and it will be given to you."

(Matthew 7:7)

At times I have become frustrated with some people when discussing the relationship issue. When I've mentioned that I'm single and I would like to be married, they have answered with some platitude like, "Well, just ask God" or "Pray about it." As if I had somehow not thought of doing this for all these years, and completely neglected to pray to God about the situation!

I talk to God about it all the time. Sometimes I'm tired of talking to Him about it. At times I have wondered if He's tired of hearing me talk to Him about it! But I have asked because He has told me to ask Him for what I need:

"Ask and it will be given to you."

(Matthew 7:7)

So I continue to ask. However, it has not always been as easy as that.

Others have said to me, "Not everyone is meant to be married..." The implication being, if it's not happened for you by now, it probably won't, so just accept you're gonna be single for the rest of your life and live with it!

Are they right? How can I know if a long wait is just that – a long wait – or if it's actually a "no"? Am I just burying my head in the sand by asking and believing God to provide a husband for me?

I don't think so.

It is a desire of my heart that I believe God is able to fulfil for me.

Jesus said in Matthew 7:9-11,

"Which of you, if his son asks for bread, will give him a stone? Or if he asks for a fish, will give him a snake? If you then, though you are evil, know how to give good gifts to your children, how much more will your Father in heaven give good gifts to those who ask Him!"

God knows the difference between being single and married. So if I've asked Him for a husband, why am I still single?

I don't know.

What I do know is that it's a difficult situation to live with. There are multiple dilemmas to consider. What do I do?

As I've gotten older, I've become aware that it is increasingly difficult to meet single men in church who are nearer my age. Unfortunately, there do not appear to be as many single men in church as there are single women.

What about the situation of the older man who has never been married? Considering the ratio of men to women in church, one might imagine he would be spoilt for choice. So why is *he* not married? Does he have issues? Is he expecting his wife to be his mother? Is he avoiding taking on further responsibility in life? Will he be able to stand firm as a rock to support his wife and children through thick and thin? Will he be too stuck in his ways to embrace the give and take that's needed in a relationship?

What about the man who is divorced? From a biblical standpoint, should he be able to remarry? What about his emotional baggage? Has he healed from that? Is he able to develop a healthy relationship in the future and be willing to resolve difficulties before they escalate? Will past problems resurface in a new relationship?

Then there is the issue of step-children. Is it possible to be the step-mother to a man's children and not be seen as the wicked stepmom?

How would the new family dynamic be handled? What involvement would the "Ex" have with him and the children? How would that affect the new relationship?

If both parties have children, how will this new family combination blend?

To "just ask" sounds simple enough, but as an older woman wanting to get married, what exactly am I asking for in this world of complex relationships that we live in? Modern relationships seem like such a minefield that it would be easier not to bother with marriage at all.

I have heard some married people say, "You're better off single. It's better than being in a bad relationship!" Of course, I don't want to be in a bad relationship – who would choose to pursue a bad relationship rather than a good one?

But do I see the majority of people choosing to go through life single and childless? No! If that was the case then the human race would have been extinct a long time ago. Wouldn't most people prefer to be in a good marriage than be single?

It doesn't help when people oversimplify the situation. Many just don't recognise – and almost trivialise – the depth of emotional pain I feel as a single woman. To be glad that I'm not stuck in a bad marriage is no consolation for being single. I could be in a good marriage! Not all marriages are bad, are they?

So I am asking God for a good husband and to help me to be a good wife.

Another challenge is seeing women who've been single for a while getting married. At times, people have said to me, "I prayed and God answered me." Sometimes I get jealous.

I ask God, "Why don't you answer me too?" It's difficult to cope when you see other women showing off their ring finger with a huge wedding ring, and later popping out babies. If I'm honest, it can make me feel bitter and twisted, but that is not the person I want to be. So I ask God to forgive me and help me be happy for those who've received the gift of marriage and the blessing of babies.

I know I'm not alone in feeling miserable sometimes when things don't work out as I'd hoped; when people are insensitive and my feelings are crushed.

Read the story of Hannah in 1 Samuel chapter one, for instance.

Hannah was married to Elkanah, but she could not have children. He had another wife, Peninnah, who had borne sons and daughters for him, but he really loved Hannah and would always give her a double portion of meat when they went to sacrifice at Shiloh. Peninnah would provoke Hannah and irritate her – no doubt making her feel like nothing, since she had no children.

Though he loved her deeply, even Elkanah didn't understand the depths of despair that Hannah felt. He asked her, *"Don't I mean more to you than ten sons?"* But his words couldn't console her. We read that Hannah's anguish continued for *"year after year"* and that *"she wept and would not eat"* (1 Samuel 1:7, 8). How awful for Hannah. She had such deep pain and sorrow, collected over years of asking God for a child and not receiving one.

"In bitterness of soul Hannah wept much and prayed to the Lord ... 'Look upon your servant's misery and remember me.'"

(1 Samuel 1:10-11)

Hannah's story gives me some encouragement because I

realise that I am not alone. Someone else has experienced similar heartfelt pain. I know I'm not alone in feeling forgotten by God, after going through this misery for years.

Like Hannah, it's not that I'm not getting on with living my life – I'm keeping busy, working, helping others, doing projects and carrying out my day-to-day responsibilities. It's just that this situation hasn't changed and never goes away. It cannot be forgotten because I'm living with it; I face it every day at some point. It's like going through a day and missing a meal. Although you forgot to eat at the time, you soon remember when you feel the hunger pangs and your stomach starts to growl! Somehow, something or someone always reminds me that I'm alone.

Hannah was so distressed about her situation, silently pouring her heart out to the Lord, that Eli the priest thought she was drunk. As she prayed her lips were moving but her voice wasn't heard. When he accused her of drinking, Hannah replied,

"I have been praying here out of my great anguish and grief."

(1 Samuel 1:16)

Even though Hannah's "church pastor" didn't understand what she was going through, she was able to express it to God. I admire Hannah because she did not give up hope, despite receiving ridicule, provocation, and being misunderstood. She kept asking God. Eventually, we read that,

"The Lord remembered her and in the course of time Hannah conceived and gave birth to a son. She named him Samuel, saying, 'Because I asked the Lord for him.'"

(1 Samuel 1:19-20)

I need to learn from Hannah. God said "ASK" and I need to keep on asking for my husband. I believe that one day the Lord will remember me, and I will be able to say, "I asked the Lord for him."

Reflect:
When you are in pain and the situation looks bad, keep talking to your Father God. He hears and answers.

Meditate:
"Until now you have not asked for anything in my name. Ask and you will receive, and your joy will be complete."

(John 16:24)

"For surely, O Lord, you bless the righteous; you surround them with your favour as with a shield."

(Psalm 5:12)

"Then you will call, and the Lord will answer; you will cry for help, and He will say 'Here am I.'"

(Isaiah 58:9)

Pray:
Write a prayer to your Heavenly Father and tell Him how you feel: Tell Him about any frustration, anxiety or anger you may be experiencing and ask Him to help you to keep trusting Him.

Chapter Six
WAITING AND BELIEVING

"Blessed is she who has believed that what the Lord has said to her will be accomplished!"

(Luke 1:45, NIV 1982 Ed.)

"After this his wife Elizabeth became pregnant and for five months remained in seclusion. 'The Lord has done this for me,; she said. 'In these days He has shown His favour and taken away my disgrace among the people.'"

(Luke 1:24-25)

Elizabeth was barren; she could not have children (Luke 1:7). Worse still, she and her husband, Zechariah, were now old. They were past it. Zechariah said as much to the angel Gabriel:

"I am an old man and my wife is well on in years."

(Luke 1:18)

Basically, he was saying, "It's all over. It's too late for us."

But what seems impossible to us is not impossible with God. God sent Gabriel to tell Zechariah that after all these years of waiting their prayers had been heard. They would have a son!

"The angel said to him, 'Do not be afraid Zechariah; your prayer has been heard. Your wife Elizabeth will bear a son, and

you are to give him the name John. He will be a joy and delight to you and many will rejoice because of his birth."

(Luke 1:13-14)

How amazing to hear such great news! Had God really heard? Now, at this late stage He was going to answer? As far as Zechariah knew, this was physically impossible. Not even Viagra could help him now! And more than likely Elizabeth had already gone through the menopause. Wasn't God a bit too late? Zechariah doubted God.

When we can't see things from our human perspective, we tend to think that they must therefore be impossible. We judge God according to our human limitations. But God is not limited by earthly constraints. He is the Creator of all things. He is the one who made things appear out of nothing. Who are we to tell God, "It's too late for me"?

I have been pleasantly uplifted and encouraged by several weddings over the past few years. One lady told me that her greatest joy was seeing her daughter get married recently. Her daughter had been in a number of relationships that hadn't worked out, and struggled to raise her children in difficult circumstances. Finally she placed herself back onto a path of success by being where God wanted her. Then, after praying and waiting for such a long time to have a husband, God answered her prayer in her late 40's. The whole family was overjoyed.

Sometimes, because we have waited so long for an answer, we give up hope and stop believing that God even hears our prayers. I imagine that Zechariah and Elizabeth had been married for years, wanting a child but never getting one, until they gave up hope of ever having one. They just accepted they would have to bear the "disgrace" of being childless; that was their lot.

How painfully disappointing to be full of hope and have

that hope crushed; for it to simply fade away as the years went by; to be so bereft of hope that even when we hear the promise of good news, we can't fully believe it.

What proof did Zechariah have that this was for real? Poor man, he of little faith. His human frailty couldn't grapple with the revelation that he and Elizabeth were expecting a baby at their age. As a result, God made him mute. He would remain speechless until the baby was born.

I know many people who want to get married but have lost hope, feeling that it's never going to happen. It can be a challenge to keep on believing when nothing is changing.

I have felt the stigma of being single and childless as though it's some kind of disease. The sideways looks, the raised eyebrows…

"You're not married yet?! What are you waiting for?"

It still hurts to hear such comments. Do people think I have purposely chosen this for myself?

At those times I cry out, "God where are you? Have you been hearing my prayers for the past 16 years?"

When there is no visible sign of change, we find it hard to believe God will ever answer positively.

For many people singleness is a huge struggle on many different levels. We all start off single and that's a great time for learning about yourself and discovering how to take on responsibilities in life. At some point we may consider what kind of life we would like to have and maybe plan how we can achieve it. Everyone is different. Some people prefer not to make plans.

I wanted to get my education, qualifications, have a good job, establish my career and see the world. I wanted God to guide my life and work. Having a life that I enjoyed was important. I wanted to take the opportunity to do things that women in previous generations, like my grandmother, hadn't been able to do because of financial constraints, family responsibilities, and a lack of resources.

I was growing up in a time where women had more access to opportunities in further/higher education, jobs and travel, leisure, and leadership. Getting married and having a family was something I wanted, but it wasn't the only thing I wanted. Doing that later on, in my thirties, was what I had in mind. So for me, singleness was great in my teens, twenties and early thirties. But in my late thirties, it was a bit shocking to find that my expectation of marriage had not materialised – and it was way past the time schedule I had envisaged.

I thought I had been waiting in a positive way: I had a busy life, work, interests, I volunteered at church and in the community on various projects, I was a sociable person … so what was going on? Why hadn't things worked out as I'd hoped?

Waiting can be lonely, especially when you desire companionship, tenderness, intimacy and sex – and these feelings cannot be expressed in the way we would like. It is also difficult when you feel like the odd one out because your friends are married with children and you are not. Sometimes they go out as couples and you don't fit into that equation. Once you were all friends together, but now they are married the situation has changed. It can feel a little awkward at times – as if you don't belong or have overstayed your welcome.

Isolation can set in. Sometimes I just found it easier to stay at home on my own. Who am I going to go out with anyway? Things have changed. My circles of "going out" friends have diminished. They have families now, the responsibilities of a husband and children, not much time to go out and socialise. Or if they do go out, it will be a huge effort to organise the home, the kids, and the husband. They are tired just thinking about it; it is hardly worth the effort!

Waiting can affect our attitude and self-esteem. We may have started out positive, but the longer we wait, the more we descend into the valley of moaning. I know, I complained about my situation until I was tired of hearing myself! I questioned what was going on and why I had to wait so long. Remember the waiting room scenario? How was I going to wait? Was I going to wait patiently or not?

I was brought back to God's Word.

"But Zion said 'the Lord has forsaken me; the Lord has forgotten me' ... 'I will not forget you! See, I have engraved you on the palm of my hands' ... 'Then you will know that I am the Lord; those who hope in me will not be disappointed.'"

(Isaiah 49:14-16, 23)

"I am still confident of this; I will see the goodness of the Lord in the land of the living. Wait for the Lord; be strong and take heart and wait for the Lord."

(Psalm 27:13-14)

I have found that God's Word provides help for me during the times when I don't feel anyone understands how I'm feeling. He reassures me that He does understand and I will not be disappointed by the outcome He has planned for me, if I wait on Him to work things out.

I thank God for showing me that He has mercy even when I doubt Him.

God didn't change His mind about giving Zechariah a son because of his doubts. He fulfilled His promise and both he and Elizabeth were full of joy to have their baby. A miracle child!

God is not finished with miracles in our time either. He can provide miracle spouses and miracle babies. Let us keep praying and stay faithful while we wait. Who knows what God will do next for you and me?

Reflect:

Waiting is not easy, but God will give you the strength to be patient and positive.

Meditate:

"Though the fig tree does not bud and there are no grapes on the vines, though the olive crop fails and the fields produce no food, though there are no sheep in the pen and no cattle in the stalls, yet I will rejoice in the Lord, I will be joyful in God my Saviour. The Sovereign Lord is my strength; He makes my feet like the feet of deer, He enables me to go on the heights."

(Habakkuk 3:17-19)

"But if we hope for what we do not yet have, we wait for it patiently. In the same way, the Spirit helps us in our weakness. We do not know what we ought to pray for, but the Spirit himself intercedes for us with groans that words cannot express. And He who searches our hearts knows the mind of the Spirit, because the Spirit intercedes for the saints in accordance with God's will."

(Romans 8:25-27)

"This is what the Lord says: 'In the time of my favour I will answer you.'"

(Isaiah 49:8)

"Submit to God and be at peace with Him; in this way prosperity will come to you. Accept instructions from His mouth and lay up His word in your heart."

(Job 22:21-22)

Pray:

Write a prayer to your Heavenly Father and tell Him how you feel.
Ask for the strength, peace and joy you need in times of waiting:

CHAPTER SEVEN
WHAT'S WRONG WITH ME?

"Thank you for making me so wonderfully complex! It is amazing to think about. Your workmanship is marvellous – and how well I know it."

(Psalm 139:14, TLB)

Have you read the story of the Samaritan woman and Jesus at the well? You can find it in John chapter 4 in The Living Bible:

"He had to go through Samaria on the way, and around noon as he approached the village of Sychar, he came to Jacob's well, located on the parcel of ground Jacob gave to his son Joseph. Jesus was tired from the long walk in the hot sun and sat wearily beside the well.

Soon a Samaritan woman came to draw water, and Jesus asked her for a drink. He was alone at the time as his disciples had gone into the village to buy some food. The woman was surprised that a Jew would ask a 'despised Samaritan' for anything—usually they wouldn't even speak to them!—and she remarked about this to Jesus.

He replied, 'If you only knew what a wonderful gift God has for you, and who I am, you would ask me for some living water!'

'But you don't have a rope or a bucket,' she said, 'and this is a very deep well! Where would you get this living water? And besides, are you greater than our ancestor Jacob? How can you offer better water than this which he and his sons and cattle enjoyed?'

Jesus replied that people soon became thirsty again after drinking this water. 'But the water I give them,' he said, 'becomes a perpetual spring within them, watering them forever with eternal life.'

'Please, sir,' the woman said, 'give me some of that water! Then I'll never be thirsty again and won't have to make this long trip out here every day.'

'Go and get your husband,' Jesus told her.

'But I'm not married,' the woman replied.

'All too true!' Jesus said. 'For you have had five husbands, and you aren't even married to the man you're living with now.'

'Sir,' the woman said, 'you must be a prophet.' ...

... The woman said, 'Well, at least I know that the Messiah will come—the one they call Christ—and when he does, he will explain everything to us.'

Then Jesus told her, 'I am the Messiah!'

Just then his disciples arrived. They were surprised to find him talking to a woman, but none of them asked him why, or what they had been discussing.

Then the woman left her water pot beside the well and went back to the village and told everyone, 'Come and meet a man who told me everything I ever did! Can this be the Messiah?' So the people came streaming from the village to see him.

Meanwhile, the disciples were urging Jesus to eat. 'No,' he said, 'I have some food you don't know about.'

'Who brought it to him?' the disciples asked each other.

Then Jesus explained: 'My nourishment comes from doing the will of God who sent me, and from finishing his work.' ...

... Many from the Samaritan village believed he was the Messiah because of the woman's report: 'He told me everything I ever did!' When they came out to see him at the well, they begged him to stay at their village; and he did, for two days, long enough for many of them to believe in him after hearing him. Then they said to the woman, 'Now we believe because we have heard him ourselves, not just because of what you told us.

He is indeed the Saviour of the world.'"

(John 4:4-42, TLB)

John 4:6-7 points out that the Samaritan woman came to the well to get water at 12 noon. That wasn't the normal time of day for collecting water. She didn't want to go to the well early in the morning when the other women would be drawing water. Instead, she went when no one was around, hiding from the world, not wanting to be seen, not wanting people to know about her secret life.

She was living with a man and they weren't married. Because she'd had five previous husbands, the shame and stigma of those failed relationships dogged her. It wasn't something she wanted to talk about with anyone. I can imagine her thinking after yet another relationship breakdown, "What's wrong with me? Why didn't this relationship work?"

Jesus knew all about her past and present, yet He did not seek to judge or condemn her. Instead He wanted to meet her deepest need – one that she may not even have recognised. She needed a Saviour to save her from herself – from her lifestyle – and to give her the hope of a better tomorrow. She was seeking something "better" in all the wrong places.

What a situation to be in – meeting a strange man at a well. Yet somehow this sounds familiar. Rebecca met Abraham and Isaac's servant at a well and she later became Isaacs's wife. Jacob met his future wife, Rachel, at a well. His love for her was so great that he worked for 14 years so that she could be his wife.

Isaac and Jacob turned out to be good husbands. The Samaritan woman, however, had had a string of failed relationships. Men came and went in her life, leaving her still feeling dissatisfied, empty and thirsting for fulfilment.

How many times in the past had she come to that well

to draw water, going about her usual daily household duties? It was the same old thing today. The same, but different. This man Jesus was different. And what He offered her was considerably more than any man could ever give: eternal life and fulfilment.

"Jesus replied that people soon became thirsty again after drinking this water. 'But the water I give them,' he said, 'becomes a perpetual spring within them, watering them forever with eternal life.'"

(v13-14)

How many times have I been hopeful that this time, the relationship will be different; that I'll find the happiness I've been looking for? Things looked promising at first – going on dates, talking on the phone, chilling out together – but sooner or later things changed.

How many times have I wondered, "What is wrong with me? What did I do wrong? Is it something I said? Is it the way I look? Is there something that puts a man off me? Is it that I'm too direct and speak my mind? Or not direct enough? Am I too willing to please? Do I appear needy? Or seem desperate? Or cold or…?"

I have many questions but no answers.

I recall one relationship that I thought was going well until the issue of sex before marriage came up. I didn't want to have sex, but he kept trying to go down that road, and we had a difference of opinion. Why couldn't he understand? I thought he would. After all, we were both Christians.

But the flesh is weak. Wanting to love and be loved, desiring some TLC, little by little I compromised my position. Somehow I didn't really feel any happier. Deep down I felt worse. Maybe what we were doing wasn't actually "having sex", but it was sexualised behaviour. How far was I willing to go and what was I willing to do to be "happy"? Yes, I had needs and desires, but I was not fulfilling God's will for my life this way, so how could I find true happiness by knowingly continuing on this path?

Jesus later told His disciples after meeting the woman at the well,

"My nourishment comes from doing the will of God who sent me, and from finishing his work."

(v34)

I think about that statement in relation to my life and situation. Jesus understands our needs and desires because He was a man. He experienced hunger and tiredness just like us. He experienced temptation. Yet He knew that He was here to do the will of God, and this came first. It was what nourished and fulfilled Him. Doing God's will needs to bring me happiness too.

But, I was at war with myself and I couldn't reconcile this. It was either I please myself and don't please God, or I please God and don't please myself. It was a difficult choice, a huge struggle, especially when every part of me – except my spirit – was screaming out to have its own way. Thank God that on this occasion the spirit won. However, this is not always the case. I have made many bad choices in my life. It is a constant battle to do the right thing.

In this relationship, I had to face making a tough decision. Could we find a way to resolve things between us in order for the relationship to work? Sadly not. It turned out that we both wanted different things and were not ultimately heading in the same direction. We broke up. It was very painful.

Like the woman at the well, I felt the shame and stigma of yet another failed relationship. "What's wrong with me? Why can't I be in a relationship that works out? How hard can this be?! I meet a guy ... we get along really well ... I love him ... he loves me ... we get married. Isn't it supposed to be that simple? Or am I stupid enough to think that it is? I know relationships are not easy, but they can work.

Although I am seeking "the one", there is still the need for a deeper, more meaningful relationship that will endure the ups and downs of my life. I want to be filled with a joy that is not dependent on my situation. Only God's love can do this. I know that I am loved despite my past bad decisions, despite my failed relationships, despite my low self-esteem, despite me not having the prettiest, longest legs, the most pert behind or voluptuous bosom, and despite my panda eyes...

I just want to be loved, truly loved.

I realise that I need the constant reassurance of God's love for me. He does love me. I know it in my head. I see it in the words on the pages of the Bible. But often I do not feel it in my heart. It's tragic, but true. I often have to repeat these words over and over again, just to convince myself of His love for me.

"I have loved you with an everlasting love; I have drawn you with loving kindness."

(Jeremiah 31:3)

I feel like the woman at the well. I've been seeking love and not finding it. Time and time again facing disappointment and pain. At times I feel like an outcast, rejected and abandoned. I need my Saviour's healing touch, for Him to give me that "living water", His Spirit of love. An everyday reminder – a reminder every minute, if necessary – to give me renewed hope and confidence of His great love for me. It is by believing that He loves me, that I can also believe that I am loveable and that there is nothing wrong with me after all.

Reflect:
God knows that you're not perfect, no one is, and He loves you so much. Ask Him to fill your heart with His love.

Meditate:
"But God demonstrated His own love for us in this: while we were still sinners, Christ died for us."

(Romans 5:8)

"Forget the former things; do not dwell on the past. See, I am doing a new thing! Now it springs up; do you not perceive it? I am making a way in the desert and streams in the wasteland ... To give drink to my people, my chosen, the people I formed for myself that they may proclaim my praise."

(Isaiah 43:18-21)

"Peace I leave with you; my peace I give you ... do not let your heart be troubled and do not be afraid."

(John 14:27)

Pray:
Write a prayer to your Heavenly Father and tell Him how you feel: Thank Him for your life. Ask Him to fill you with His love each day so you can carry out His purpose for your life.

Chapter Eight

THE FOUR D'S

"But blessed is the one who trusts in the Lord, whose confidence is in Him. They will be like a tree planted by the water that sends out its roots by the stream. It does not fear when the heat comes, its leaves are always green. It has no worries in a year of drought and never fails to bear fruit."

(Jeremiah 17:7-8, NIV)

Do we really know ourselves? How well do you know yourself?

I am convinced that we sometimes live in denial of the truth about ourselves. We don't fully understand how we will react to certain situations until we are faced with them. How will we handle difficult, disappointing, frightening, shocking or distressing circumstances? What will happen to us emotionally? Look at this incident from Matthew 14:23-33, New International Version:

"After he had dismissed them, he went up on a mountainside by himself to pray. Later that night, he was there alone, and the boat was already a considerable distance from land, buffeted by the waves because the wind was against it. Shortly before dawn Jesus went out to them, walking on the lake.

When the disciples saw him walking on the lake, they were terrified.

'It's a ghost,' they said, and cried out in fear.

But Jesus immediately said to them: 'Take courage! It is I. Don't be afraid.'

'Lord, if it's you,' Peter replied, 'tell me to come to you on the water.'

'Come,' he said.

Then Peter got down out of the boat, walked on the water and came toward Jesus. But when he saw the wind, he was afraid and, beginning to sink, cried out, 'Lord, save me!'

Immediately Jesus reached out his hand and caught him. 'You of little faith,' he said, 'why did you doubt?' And when they climbed into the boat, the wind died down.

Then those who were in the boat worshiped him, saying, 'Truly you are the Son of God.'"

What a privilege the disciples had to be in the company of Jesus and to learn from Him, directly, every day! As we read about their situation we see how Jesus took time to be alone to pray, so that He could be prepared and strengthened for whatever winds or storms He had to face in life.

The disciples were caught up in the wind on the lake. Then, when faced with what they thought was a "ghost" walking towards them on the water, they were terrified! We are talking about twelve big grown men being petrified!

We may think we are more than able to handle a crisis, or challenging situations, but when faced with them we crumble – we're afraid, terrified, unable to cope. At such times of distress we need to hear the familiar, comforting voice of our friend, Jesus, telling us that He is with us, so we need not be afraid.

Big mouth Peter asks Jesus if he can come to Him and Jesus agrees, so Peter steps out of the boat and walks on the water towards Jesus. Then he sees the wind blowing the waves and begins to sink! He calls out to Jesus in fear and Jesus immediately holds him and saves him. Wow! Saved by the hand of Jesus. Jesus caught him before he sunk under the water and drowned.

No matter what kind of deep water we are in, no matter how strong the winds are blowing against us, we can guarantee that Jesus will be there to comfort us, give us courage, and hold us up and save us. We must call Him.

If we are in need of medical assistance, the police or the fire department, we call 999 to get help. We must learn to call on Jesus, just as He continually called on His Father when He prayed on the mountain. Through prayer we too can receive strength to deal with our situations, whether it's in advance or while we are going through them.

Jesus knows that sometimes our faith is small and weak, and that we suffer from doubt.

I can hardly believe the depths of emotional pain I've experienced over the years in dealing with singleness in my late thirties and forties. I never felt that way in my teens, twenties or early thirties. Things were generally fine and fun. I was enjoying being single, going on dates, having relationships when the opportunity arose.

Battling "the four D's" was not a part of my experience then, like it is now. I call them Disappointment, Distress, Despair and Depression.

Disappointment:

When our hopes and expectations are not fulfilled we feel disappointed. Disappointment is part of life and we will all face it at some time. Things do not always turn out as we had hoped. Receiving a knock-back may be an opportunity for us to develop resilience, to keep positive, be hopeful and determined, to look forward to future success. But if we experience a number of disappointments, that can have the effect of knocking us down. Over time, it leaves us with little or no strength to get up. In my experience, this can lead to distress.

Distress:

This has been defined as the feeling of great pain, anxiety, or sorrow; acute physical or mental suffering. I have to admit that there have been times when my sadness and emotional pain were worse than any physical pain I'd felt before. I tried to fight it, but at times it was overwhelming. It was as though I was in a dark cave, with no light, no way out that I could see.

What bothered me so much to make me feel this way?

The fear that I would live the rest of my life alone – which is not what I want and not how I expected my life to be. I remember when I was a child, there was an elderly lady who lived nearby. She had never married and had no children. She lived alone, but had about 20 cats! We used to call her the "cat lady". Was this to become my life?

The fear of not being able to have children. The older I became, the less time I felt I had to meet someone compatible with me, marry them and have children. Each of these stages of a relationship takes time. I didn't think time was on my side. Having babies later in life, at 40+, carries certain risks. It has been said that there is higher risk of problems and possible birth defects.

I found these thoughts painful and difficult to accept. I struggled between thinking, "This is your reality, so live with it" and thinking, "I believe that God can change this situation, so I should stay hopeful."

As the years rolled by and there was no change, however, the disappointment and distress turned to despair.

Despair:
I suffered a sense of hopelessness. I lost hope. I would try to believe that God loved me and still cared about my situation, because I could see this in other areas of my life – I had good health, a home, a job, friends, family, I was active and socialised, I was able to help others. I was blessed, yet somehow I felt cursed because I was not married. At times the pain of that would just block out all the good things. This made me feel as though I was being ungrateful, which led to feelings of guilt. It was like one load was being added to another. Depression set in.

Depression:

Most people understand depression as feeling sad, gloomy, dejected and downcast. "Pressed down" is another description that is used. I was so oppressed by heavy thoughts for so long that I felt my heart couldn't take any more. This was not how I wanted to live. I couldn't cope with these painful feelings. At times I just wanted it all to end.

I didn't want to live like this anymore.

As a Christian, how could I even think that way? Where was my faith? Didn't I believe that God loved me? At times I doubted that He cared for me and my situation. This led to more sadness, guilt and pain.

I believe the evil one will use anything to destroy. One of his main strategies is to get us to lose hope in God and doubt His love for us. He wants us to look at our problems, to see our situation as hopeless, to stay down and oppressed instead of looking upwards, towards the hope we have in God. Yet our Father God is the light of the world, the One who can dispel the darkness in our lives and bring us joy and love.

It helped me to have friends and family who I could talk to about some of the things I was going through at the time. And there was a point at which I realised I needed the help of a counsellor for support – someone who was neutral. However, the only way I could get through on a daily basis was by reminding myself of God's love for me, and focusing on His ability to make impossible things possible. I encouraged my spirit with His Word. I realised I needed to wait patiently and keep hoping in His promises. The more I looked for words of encouragement the more I found. They had a way of touching the sensitive part of me that was in pain and helped to bring healing to my emotions and spirit. Read these words from Isaiah:

"Therefore the Lord will wait, that he may be gracious to you; and therefore He will be exalted, that He may have mercy on

you. For the Lord is a God of justice; blessed are all those who wait for Him."

(Isaiah 30:18)

"You shall weep no more; He will be very gracious to you at the sound of your cry; when He hears it, He will answer you. And though the Lord gives you the bread of adversity, and the water of affliction, yet your teachers will not be moved into a corner any more, but your eyes shall see your teachers; your ears shall hear a word behind you saying, 'This is the way, walk in it,' whenever you turn to the right hand or whenever you turn to the left."

(Isaiah 30:19-21, NKJV)

I really love this passage and I think it is brought to life even more in the Amplified Bible:

"And therefore the Lord [earnestly] waits [expecting, looking, and longing] to be gracious to you; and therefore He lifts Himself up, that He may have mercy on you and show loving-kindness to you. For the Lord is a God of justice. Blessed (happy, fortunate, to be envied) are all those who [earnestly] wait for Him, who expect and look and long for Him [for His victory, His favour, His love, His peace, His joy, and His matchless, unbroken companionship]!

… you will weep no more. He will surely be gracious to you at the sound of your cry; when He hears it, He will answer you.

And though the Lord gives you the bread of adversity and the water of affliction, yet your Teacher will not hide Himself any more, but your eyes will constantly behold your Teacher. And your ears will hear a word behind you, saying, 'This is the way; walk in it,' when you turn to the right hand and when you turn to the left."

(Isaiah 30:18-21, AMP)

"O Lord be gracious unto us; we have waited for thee. Be thou their arm every morning, our salvation also in the time of trouble."

(Isaiah 33:2)

"Strengthen those who have tired hands and encourage those who have weak knees. Say to those with fearful hearts, 'Be strong, and do not fear, for your God is coming to destroy your enemies. He is coming to save you.'"

(Isaiah 35:3-4, NLT)

The Word speaks of God's plan to be gracious to you and me. He is waiting, so that when He decides to act in our situation His name will be exalted. There will be no doubt about what He has done.

God loves us, He hears our cry, He knows when we weep. But He also wants us to learn the lessons that will build and develop our character. Sometimes He is using our situation to teach us valuable, life-changing truths. Here are a few things I have discovered:

1. That waiting is a learning opportunity, not a punishment.
2. That I need to focus on God, not the things that are making me afraid of my future.
3. That I need to believe that He is with me and will save me. I can trust His word on that, so I need to be strong and not be afraid when trouble comes.
4. That I must expect good things from God in my life. Even

when things don't look good, God is able to bring about good from them.

"All things work together and are fitting into a plan for good to those who love God and are called according to His purpose"

(Romans 8:28)

5. That even when I'm scared, trembling and crying, when my circumstances don't seem to be visibly changing, and may even look like they're getting worse, I still must not give up on God. I must rejoice in the Lord, because He is my strength.

"I heard and my (whole inner self) trembled; my lips quivered at the sound. Rottenness enters into my bones and under me (down to my feet); I tremble. I will wait quietly for the day of trouble and distress when there shall come up against (my) people him who is about to invade and oppress them. Though the fig tree does not blossom and there is not fruit on the vines, (though) the product of the olive fails and the fields yield no food, though the flock is cut off from the fold and there are no cattle in the stalls, yet I will rejoice in the Lord; I will exult in the (victorious) God of my salvation! The Lord God is my strength, my personal bravery, and my invincible army; He makes my feet like hinds feet and will make me to walk (not to stand still in terror, but to walk) and make (spiritual) progress upon my high places (of trouble, suffering, or responsibility)!"

(Habakkuk 3:16-19, AMP)

To be able to rejoice when we are suffering or in trouble, I don't think is humanly possible. It takes divine strength to enable us to do it. As Habakkuk wrote, *"The Lord God is my strength."* He gives us the power to walk through the darkness and gives us light for our way.

"Who among you fears the Lord … Let the one who walks in the dark, who has no light, trust in the name of the Lord, and rely on their God."

(Isaiah 50:10, NIV)

In my situation I felt as though I was blind, in total darkness, hopeless. I thank God for being my rescuer. He showed me that He understood my pain and sorrow. He didn't condemn me for my state of mind, but had mercy on me. He saw my tears and weeping. He had pity on my fears. He was gracious, held me close to Himself, and led me into the light. As I read His Word and His promises, I believed they were for me. I took them to heart. I could trust in Him again and lean on Him for strength and comfort. God gave me renewed hope.

"He gave power to the faint; and to them that have no might He increased strength. Even the youths shall faint and be weary, and the young men shall utterly fall; but they that wait upon the Lord shall renew their strength; they shall mount up with wings as eagles; they shall run and not be weary; and they shall walk and not faint."

(Isaiah 40:29-31)

Reflect:
Trust God. He will provide comfort and healing for your pain. Talk to Him and also to trusted people and counsellors.

Meditate:
"Then maidens will dance and be glad, young men and old as

well. I will turn their mourning into gladness; I will give them comfort and joy instead of sorrow."

(Jeremiah 31:13)

"When I am afraid, I will trust in you. In God, whose word I praise, in God I trust; I will not be afraid..."

(Psalms 56:3-4)

"Then they cried to the Lord in their trouble, and he saved them from their distress. He brought them out of darkness and the deepest gloom and broke away their chains. Let them give thanks to the Lord for His unfailing love and His wonderful deeds for men."

(Psalm 107:13-15)

"Nevertheless, I will bring health and healing ... I will heal my people and will let them enjoy abundant peace and security."

(Jeremiah 33:6)

Pray:
Write a prayer to your Heavenly Father and tell Him how you feel. Ask Him to heal you of any emotional pain and heartache you may have:

Chapter Nine
A QUESTION OF FAITH

"Because God has said, 'Never will I leave you;
never will I forsake you.' So we say with confidence,
'The Lord is my helper; I will not be afraid.'"

(Hebrews 13:5-6)

In response to my relationship dilemma some people have said to me, "Ask God for what you need and expect to receive it. Have faith."

My response to that has been that I do have faith – and I'm still waiting. I have also been told to have MORE faith. So is the issue my lack of faith then?

I don't think so.

I know I serve a powerful God, the Creator of heaven and earth. Nothing is too hard for Him. Therefore I'm sure finding a husband for me is not beyond His capability.

I recall in Genesis 24 where Abraham asked his chief servant to go to his relatives to find a wife for his son Isaac (Genesis 24:2-4). Abraham was confident that God would do this.

"The Lord, the God of heaven, who brought me out of my fathers' household and my native land and who spoke to me and promised me on oath, saying 'To your offspring I will give this land.' He will send His angels before you so that you can get a wife for my son from there."

(Genesis 24:7)

The servant also asked of God, "O Lord, God of my master Abraham, give me success today, and show kindness to my master Abraham."

(Genesis 24:12)

Not only did he pray, he received an answer immediately!!

"Before he had finished praying, Rebekah came out with her jar on her shoulder."

(Genesis 24:15)

It turned out that Rebekah was one of Abraham's relatives and both she and her family were happy to agree to the marriage. They believed that;

"This is from the Lord..."

(Genesis 24:50)

God heard the request and answered it straight away. So why wouldn't He do that for me? It's very difficult to understand what God's plan is for my life on this issue. He obviously can … but He hasn't … Does that mean He won't? Is there something I need to do?

I can understand the dilemma that Abraham and Sarah faced before they had Isaac. They had been promised a son and yet nothing had happened. Years went by … still nothing. I can imagine Sarah thinking, "Well, it hasn't happened yet, but God did say to Abraham 'I will make you into a great nation and I will bless you.' Maybe God meant that Abraham will have a child, but not through me?"

Sarah may have had that thought again and again. Then,

when the word of the Lord came to Abraham that, "*...a son coming from your own body will be your heir*" (Genesis 15:4), maybe she was convinced that it was not her who was going to give birth.

Abraham believed God (Genesis 15:6), but after ten years of waiting he went along with Sarah's suggestion to take a second wife, Hagar, Sarah's maid, and have a child with her (Genesis 16:1-4). Does that mean that Abraham and Sarah didn't have any faith? Maybe they thought God wanted them to do something to help bring the promise to fulfilment? We often do not clearly understand God's ways, or God's plan. This, and our impatience, can cause us to take matters in our own hands and make a mess in the process. Things are not always as simple as we would like them to be. Or maybe it's really very simple – we need to leave things alone and allow God to deal with them when He's ready. In practice, that's not so easy to do.

I imagine that Abraham and Sarah's faith was severely tested over the many years of waiting. After all, Abraham was 75 years old when God told him he would make him a great nation. He had Ishmael with Hagar at age 86, and it turned out that this was not the promised child! It was when Abraham was 99 years old, 24 years after God first spoke to him, that God reminded him of what he would do in more detail.

"As for Sarai your wife ... I will bless her and will surely give you a son by her and I will bless her so that she will be the mother of nations, kings and peoples will come from her."

(Genesis 17:15-16)

Why didn't God say that earlier? Then there would have been no room for confusion; no uncertainty. These are questions that come to my finite mind and I have no direct answers.

God alone knows why He does what He does … when He does … how He does.

Even Abraham found the situation he was in funny:

"Abraham fell face down, he laughed and said to himself, 'Will a son be born to a man a hundred years old? Will Sarah bear a child at the age of 90?' And Abraham said to God 'If only Ishmael might live under your blessing!'"

(Genesis 17:17-18)

In other words, Abraham was saying, "Lord, it's really hard to believe. Let's be realistic – please bless the child I already have!"

Then God said,

"Yes … your wife Sarah will bear you a son and you will call him Isaac (which means he laughs)."

(Genesis 17:19)

Abraham was not the only one who laughed.

"Therefore Sarah laughed within herself, saying, after I am waxed old shall I have pleasure, my lord being old also? And the Lord said unto Abraham, wherefore did Sarah laugh, saying, shall I of a surety bear a child, which am old? Is anything too hard for the Lord?"

(Genesis 18:12-14)

God knew both Abraham's and Sarah's thoughts and heard both of them laugh inside. Nothing escapes God's attention. Maybe by naming the child Isaac (he laughs), God wanted to remind them of how they had laughed at the apparent impossibility of their situation – Abraham saying, "I can't be a dad at 100!" and Sarah saying, "I can't be a mum at 90!" God can hear and make the impossible possible. Yes, God can seriously do it!!!

We cannot hide our thoughts and secret longings from God. We may think one thing and say something else, but God knows what's really going on inside us. He knows the desire of our heart. I believe He wants us to trust Him to work things out, in His own way, in His own time. Our faith may be tested, like Abraham's and Sarah's, but we should not give up believing that nothing is impossible with God.

"For with God all things are possible…"

(Mark 10:27)

Reflect:
Remembering how God has helped you in the past will help you to know that He will not leave you now.

Meditate:
"Have faith in the Lord your God and you will be upheld; have faith in His prophets and you will be successful."

(2 Chronicles 20:20)

"I will remember the deeds of the Lord: yes I will remember your miracles of long ago. I will meditate on all your works and consider all your mighty deeds … You are the God who performs miracles."

(Psalm 77:11-14)

"You will keep in perfect peace those whose minds are steadfast,

because they trusts in you. Trust in the Lord forever, for the Lord, the Lord Himself, is the Rock eternal."

(Isaiah 26:3-4, NIV)

"Consider it pure joy, my brothers and sisters whenever you face trials of many kinds, because you know that the testing of your faith develops perseverance. Perseverance must finish its work so that you may be mature and complete, not lacking anything."

(James 1:2-4, NIV)

Pray:
Write a prayer to your Heavenly Father and tell Him how you feel. Thank Him for something He has done for you:

CHAPTER TEN

HOPE IN GOD

"And we know that in all things God works
for the good of those who love him, who have been called
according to his purpose."

(Romans 8:28)

I was out one day when I met my friend, Jake. He and I always have a chat and a laugh when we meet. This day he grabbed my hand and looked at it. "You not married yet?" he asked. I laughed. "No, I'm waiting for you!" I replied.

We both laughed.

As we looked at each other I thought, "We are both single ... so why not get together? He's a really cute guy and I do like him ... I've been waiting on God for sooooo looong and nothing is happening... I can't handle it! I'm lonely. I really need a companion. I'm sexually frustrated and I'd love to have a baby. Here is an opportunity to have what I want."

We chatted some more and then went our separate ways.

Later on I thought about it some more. Jake is a hard working guy, family minded, wants to be a dad, is supportive and fun loving.

But then I thought about some of his lifestyle habits – smoking, drinking, partying ... and I didn't think I could live with that.

Though he knows I'm a Christian, I can't imagine Jake would really understand how much God means to me. If I said to him, "Because of my faith in God, there's going to be no sex before marriage," I don't think that would go down too well! Jake doesn't believe in God or go to church. I doubt he would appreciate where I am coming from. He has been in a long term relationship before, living with his girlfriend for many years. I can't imagine he would be prepared to be in a sexless relationship.

I realised that whether or not a man was a Christian and attended church, I was expecting them to live by God's standards, not the world's. The world around me accepts sex before marriage and living together as normal. That is it's standard – to do otherwise seems abnormal to most non-Christians. It seems that few are prepared to live by what God says these days. I have to admit that sadly, at times, that includes me. In the past I haven't always lived according to God's expectations of me when it comes to relationships. I pleased myself and got involved with guys in ways I should not have. I knew better, but I didn't do better. I was weak. But that's no excuse really. I didn't rely on Christ to get me through.

With Jake, once again I was at a crossroads. Would I put my hope in God to provide for me or would I give up and take matters into my own hands? I hoped I'd learned from my past mistakes … I thought I'd promised myself that I wouldn't go down that road again … hadn't I decided to wait on God, because it really wasn't worth doing it any other way?

It's amazing how crazy we can get sometimes. It's not difficult to get carried away with our thoughts, so that before we know it we are behaving in ways we wouldn't have thought possible! And don't say, "It won't happen to me!" It's only by the grace of God that any of us avoid falling into all kinds of messy situations.

So I asked God to help me to not disgrace Him; to not do stuff I shouldn't do. I asked Him to help me to keep hoping in Him, despite how I felt. It wasn't easy. I struggled. But I kept hoping.

Psalm 16:1, 8-9 says,

"Preserve me, O God; for in thee do I put my trust. I have set the Lord always before me; because He is at my right hand, I shall not be moved. Therefore my heart is glad, and my glory rejoiceth; my flesh also shall rest in hope."

I needed to refocus my mind on what I knew God would want me to do. I had to keep God's expectations before me – His standards – not allowing myself to be moved from them. Previously I had slipped, due to my own weakness and desires. But this time things had to be different. How could I want God's blessing on my life, then not live by what He asks of me? I felt as though I was letting Him down; my thoughts were so weak.

When faced with difficulties, we need to encourage ourselves. At times there is no one else who can do that for us. We need to remind ourselves of God's love; that He understands our situation.

"For He hath not despised nor abhorred the affliction of the afflicted; neither hath He hid His face from him; but when he cried unto Him, He heard."

(Psalm 22:24)

I was afraid that I would give in to my feelings, so I prayed really hard for God to make me strong when I next saw my friend, so that I wouldn't be tempted to do wrong.

"O keep my soul and deliver me; let me not be ashamed; for I put my trust in thee. Let integrity and uprightness preserve me; for I wait on thee."

(Psalm 25:20, 21)

There have been dark days, when everything feels hopeless. When my hopes and dreams of having the family I want are fading fast. Is it possible that I *never will* marry? Is it possible that I will never experience giving birth to a baby? That thought alone saddens my heart and makes me want to cry. I am human and it would be painful not to have that desire met. It feels difficult to accept that God would allow that.

But I pray that I will still trust Him, knowing that, in His wisdom, He knows what's best for me. I pray that I will be able to enjoy my life and not cause any dissatisfaction I feel to damage my relationship with God. Rather than dwell on what I don't have, I prefer to live in hope and not remain in hopelessness ... but it can be a struggle.

I have a number of close friends whose weddings I have attended. They've now been married for years – some 5 or even 15 years or more! Most have children. Where has the time gone? So quickly, yet so slowly, as things change, yet remain the same for me...

I've tried not to show the sadness. And what's the point in talking about it? There is nothing anyone can do to ease my pain. I've cried myself to sleep and woken up only to cry again. I cry out to God, "Please hear me, please answer me."

"Unto thee will I cry, O lord my rock; be not silent to me; lest ... I become like them that go down into the pit. Hear the voice of my supplications, when I cry unto thee, when I lift up my hands towards thy holy oracle ... The Lord is my strength and my shield; my heart trusted in Him, and I am helped; Therefore my heart greatly rejoiceth; and with my song will I praise Him."

(Psalm 28:1-2, 7)

There is something about listening to praise songs or singing praise to God that just lifts the spirit. When I feel I'm in darkness, if I put on a Gospel CD, DVD or Christian radio, I find that my spirit is encouraged. At times the words touch so directly on my need that I cry. God has brought me healing through songs. At times I have gotten so happy that I've begun dancing around the room, singing along. It can be such an amazing transformation, from hopelessness to renewed hope and joy, because I've chosen to open my heart to God's word through music.

"Weeping may endure for a night, but joy cometh in the morning … Thou hast turned for me my mourning into dancing; thou hast put off my sackcloth, and girded me with gladness."

(Psalm 30:5, 11)

"The Lord is nigh unto them that are of a broken heart; and saveth such as be of a contrite heart."

(Psalm 34:18)

"I will bless the Lord at all times His praise shall continually be in my mouth."

(Psalm 34:1)

God knows when our heart is broken. He knows the pain and sadness we experience. He is not far away from us – He's near. He is always close by our side to comfort us and take us through the difficulties and challenges we face. Yes, we may be tempted to lose hope and give up on Him, because we think He is taking so very long to sort out what we want. But instead, let us keep trusting in His love and mercy.

"Behold, the eye of the Lord is upon them that fear Him, upon them that hope in His mercy. Our soul waiteth for the Lord. He is our help and our shield. For our hearts shall rejoice in Him, because we have trusted in His Holy Name. Let thy mercy, O

Lord, be upon us, according as we hope in thee."

(Psalm 33:18, 20-22)

Any time I'm tempted to give up hope on my situation changing, I am reminded of Abraham. He was strong in his faith in God. He believed God could do the impossible and God did fulfil His promise. If God can do it for Abraham, I believe He can do it for me.

"Who against hope believed in hope. That he might become the father of many nations, according to that which was spoken, so shall they seed be ... He staggered not at the promise of God through unbelief, but was strong in faith, giving glory to God; and being fully persuaded that, what He [God] had promised, He was able to perform."

(Romans 4:18, 20-21)

Things may seem hopeless to us, but they are not to God. Like Abraham, let us be strong in faith and *"Have faith in God"* (Mark 11:22).

Reflect:
When you need help and support, put your hope in God's Word and not in how you feel.

Meditate:
"For the Lord comforts His people and will have compassion on His afflicted ones ... I will not forget you! See, I have engraved you on the palms of my hands ... those who hope in me will not be disappointed."

(Isaiah 49:13, 15-16, 23)

"Ah, Sovereign Lord, you have made the heavens and the earth by your great power and outstretched arm. Nothing is too hard for you."

(Jeremiah 32:17)

"May the God of hope fill you with all joy and peace as you trust in him, so that you may overflow with hope by the power of the Holy Spirit."

(Romans 15:13)

Pray:
Write a prayer to your Heavenly Father and tell Him how you feel. Ask Him to comfort you and lift you up whenever you feel hopeless:

Chapter Eleven
LOOKING FORWARD

"Do not dwell on the past ... see I am doing a new thing."

(Isaiah 43:18-19)

I believe that life is full of surprises. We never know what will happen from day to day. But we do know that God loves us and has planned a good future for each of us. He desires to supply all our needs.

"But my God shall supply all your needs according to His riches in glory by Christ Jesus."

(Philippians 4:19)

I believe that if I focus on this truth, believe it, and trust Him to do it, I will find life is much better than if I feel hopeless.

During my mid-thirties, as a relationship I was in ended painfully, I took stock of my life. What should I do? I realised that I had a lot of love to give. I wanted to be in a relationship that worked, to settle down and get married. But this was not happening.

I was also at a crossroads in my career. I had pursued an area of work in mental health that I enjoyed, but I now believed it was time to move on – but to what?

After much prayer I began to see God showing me how I could take on a new role in life as a mum – a foster mum. I decided to give love to someone who needed it. It had always been a desire of my heart to foster children, whether I had my own children or not. I recognised that there was a great need for individuals and families to take the responsibility to provide love, care and a nurturing environment for children who could not be with their own family. I felt compelled to make this commitment.

Eventually I became a foster mum and was a mum to many children over the nine years that followed, until I took the big step to become a mum permanently. I adopted my last baby (he wasn't really a baby, I fostered him at the age of five and the adoption went through when he was eight years old) and deep down I knew that God had brought us together for a reason.

Giving love and support to children provided a stronger sense of purpose in my life. I felt that I was able to give back, do something to benefit others. Not only the children, but also their families, maybe even the community and society at large. Who knows how far the ripples of our help and influence can go?

Fostering children gave me an opportunity to take the focus off my situation and put my energies into nurturing another life.

It didn't take away my desire to want a husband and a birth child of my own. That was no surprise – I didn't think that it would! But I certainly felt better that I was living a more useful life and hopefully leaving a positive legacy of love.

Fostering or adoption may not be for everyone, but it is one of the best things I have done in my life and I would recommend anyone to give it serious consideration. Who knows what surprises God has for your future?

I still struggle with down times. Just recently my brother told me how beautiful I look when I smile and how frowning makes me look bad. I told him that if I wanted to frown I could and would! Yes, I was being miserable. When I'm miserable inside my face can't fake being happy for long. I can put on the mask and pretend everything is okay, grin and bear it for a time, but after a while I become exhausted. It's often easier to be alone with the sadness. I don't have to pretend to myself.

I can understand why some people prefer isolation. Not having to be around people can make our problems seem more manageable on those low days. But this approach is also counter-productive. It can spiral downwards and deteriorate into deep depression. The negative thoughts and feelings that sometimes affect me, need to be managed. Singleness is great for a time, and great for some people, but when it stops feeling great and begins to get us down, we need to find a way of addressing our feelings and coping with the situation.

We all have issues in life that we are dealing with and are affected by. Some people have physical conditions, illness, mental, emotional, environmental, relational, financial issues, and a whole range of other stuff. The issues may differ but "issues" are our common thread. Whatever they may be, we all have them.

Your issue may be different to mine. Your strength may be my weakness and vice-versa. Knowing this should help us to be more understanding and tolerant of one another. Knowing we are not perfect should help us to accept that others are imperfect too, so we should be more accepting of them. Unfortunately we don't always behave that way. Yet we all need to find a way to manage our issues and cope with life.

My mum has a physical issue with arthritis. She has swelling and pain in her knees and hands, which makes it very difficult to move around and to do everyday activities. Being in constant pain is no joke. She finds that the only way she can live is to fight the pain with painkillers; eat and drink healthy, natural foods; keep active and mobile. She is determined not to allow arthritis to stop her living the best life she can, doing things she enjoys and finding happiness in time spent with her family and friends. I admire my mum. She tries hard not to let things get her down, even though they might sometimes. She keeps fighting back.

There is a lot I can learn from her attitude to life and the problem of pain. My painful issue is singleness. It never used to be an issue, but with age, like arthritis, it has become increasingly painful, mentally and emotionally. For a long time I felt crushed by the hopelessness inside me, but God has shown me in His Word that He can heal pain. Like a painkiller, His Word brings relief. I need to apply it each time the painful thoughts, feelings and situations overwhelm me.

"For the Lord comforts His people, and will have compassion on His afflicted ones ... see, I have engraved you on the palms of My hands ... those who hope in Me will not be disappointed."

(Isaiah 49:13, 16, 23)

"The righteous cry out, and the Lord hears them; He delivers them from all their troubles. The Lord is close to the broken-hearted and saves those who are crushed in spirit."

(Psalm 34:17-18)

My mum says that she often tried to get through the day only taking one or two painkillers, even though her doctor had told her she could take up to eight! Of course, she would rather not, but at times she has had a couple more than her usual two. In the same way, I need to take a regular dose of "The Word" painkiller to deal with my situation. Unlike my mum's medication, it's not possible to overdose on God's Word. Plus it's free!

At times my mum has used a painkilling gel that she rubs

onto her painful knees. God's love, found in His Word needs to be "rubbed" into my spirit, like a healing balm, to warm my heart and soul, calm my fears. It revives my hope and faith. I really need to apply this every day.

"Cast your cares on the Lord and he will sustain you; He will never let the righteous fall."

(Psalm 55:22)

"When I am afraid, I will trust in you. In God, whose word I praise, in God I trust; I will not be afraid."

(Psalm 56:3-4)

"The Lord will guide you always; He will satisfy your needs in a sun-scorched land and will strengthen your frame. You will be like a well-watered garden, like a spring whose waters never fail."

(Isaiah 58:11)

When I meditate on verses like these, I find they help strengthen me inside and enable me to face each new day.

Here are a few things that I've considered helpful on my singleness journey that I want to share with you...

1. **Wait on God patiently and positively.** I don't like waiting in "waiting rooms", but I have learned that for me to wait patiently and positively, I need to focus on something else to make the time fly. I usually carry a book, newspaper or magazine with me. Or I use the time to plan or prepare projects I'm working on. It distracts me from the wait. I believe that, as a single person, God gives me opportunities to use my time to be a positive influence on those around

me; to do the good I can, where I am. We can all live less selfishly and give some practical help to those in need.

"I know there is nothing better for people than to be happy and do good while they live."

(Ecclesiastes 3:12, NIV)

"A generous person will prosper. Whoever refreshes others will be refreshed."

(Proverbs 11:25, NIV)

While you are waiting patiently, find ways to be generous – with your time, money and skills, with food, gifts, by encouraging others through phone calls, texts, emails. Bless others with whatever the Lord has blessed you with.

"If we hope for what we do not yet have, we wait for it patiently … in the same way, the spirit helps us in our weakness."

(Romans 8:25-26)

2. **Be hopeful.** Sometimes we are given the impression that Christians should never feel down, sad, disappointed or tired of situations. But life is full of trouble and it can affect us. We can become weak, we can fall down. But Isaiah 40:29-31 encourages me that God will renew our strength and allow us to mount up with wings like an eagle, to overcome those down times.

Meanwhile I am busy with family responsibilities, home, work, church work, projects, keeping in touch with friends. I enjoy spending time with God – reading the Word and praying –

which is a great improvement on where I used to be! I used to fall asleep midway through my conversations with God. I couldn't keep my eyes open to read a chapter of the Bible. God has helped me to grow this far, so there is hope for me to develop more. If God can help me He can help anyone.

My loneliness is specifically related to my desire for a husband to share my life with. I sometimes feel bombarded by reminders around me that say, "You're old and still single … it's too late now." This can be difficult to deal with. Seeing friends celebrating their wedding anniversary or seeing younger friends get pregnant or with their new born baby is difficult. Seeing my niece, who I held as a baby, now have children reminds me of the unfulfilled longing of my heart.

And yet, my loneliness and longing have a way of driving me back into the arms of God for more comfort, which is the best place I could be. Rather than doing something foolish that I would regret, I run back to Him and cry out for His help and strength.

"He gives power to the faint, and to them that have no might he increaseth strength. Even the youths shall faint and be weary, and the young men shall utterly fall. But they that wait upon the Lord shall renew their strength, they shall mount up with wings as eagles, they shall run and not be weary and they shall walk and not faint."

(Isaiah 40:29-31)

We need to remind ourselves of God's love for us. Say, "God loves me" and say it until you believe it! We must remember that we are loved, that God is not punishing us. He hasn't forgotten us, but has a beautiful plan that He is working out for our lives. This truth should strengthen our trust in Him, our hope that He will provide the husband we long for.

"I am like an olive tree flourishing in the house of God. I trust in God's unfailing love for ever and ever. I will praise you for ever for what you have done, in your name I will hope, for your name is good."

(Psalm 52:8-9)

An important part of not losing hope is remembering when God has been there for me in the past. Recounting those times and thanking Him for what He has already done encourages me to believe that He will answer my prayer for a husband too.

"I cried out to God to hear me. When I was in distress, I sought the Lord ... Has God forgotten to be merciful? Has He in anger withheld His compassion? Then I thought, to this I will appeal: I will remember the deeds of the Lord; yes, I will remember your miracles of long ago. I will meditate on all your works and consider all your mighty deeds .... You are the God who performs miracles."

(Psalm 77:1, 2, 9-14)

Have hope. God performs miracles!

3. Love God, your neighbour and yourself.

"Jesus said unto him, Thou shalt love the Lord thy God with all thy heart and with all they soul and with all thy mind. This is the first and great commandment and the second is like unto it. Thou shalt love thy neighbour as thyself."

(Matthew 22:37-39)

I have found that I have needed to renew my relationship

with God over the years. I decided that I needed to include Him more in my everyday life. I began to write down my prayer thoughts and talk to Him about all the issues that caused me pain. I was honest and laid it all out – my sadness, hurts, rejection, low self-esteem, feelings of being unloved and unlovable, all my fears. I cried tears of anguish and despair. At times I couldn't speak or write, all I did was cry. But I believe God read my tears and understood. I searched His Word and asked Him to reveal His love to me; to give me the encouragement I desperately needed. I've shared with you some of the verses that have strengthened me. God has become the Father I love, the One I turn to, talk to and share life's ups and downs with every day.

Loving my neighbour is something I struggle with sometimes. It's great when we can get on well with people, but there are times when we don't and that is challenging. I have to ask God to help me to be forgiving, understanding and patient with people who get on my nerves! I'm sure I get on their nerves too. But how can I say I love God if I don't love those who I see and am in contact with (1 John 4:20)? It doesn't work, so I ask God for His grace and forgiveness when I'm not the daughter He would like me to be.

I also need to love myself. This is easier for some people to do than others. If you have been abused or rejected you may find it difficult to love yourself. I have experienced rejection on many different levels in my life, and that fuelled the negative feelings I carried inside. Thinking that I was not wanted, unlovable, that there was something wrong with me, reinforced my negative thoughts and caused me to sink lower. It was a major battle to fight the rejection and love myself, but God knows our pain and gives us His love. I hold onto His promises:

"I have loved you with an everlasting love."

(Jeremiah 31:3)

"I will be a Father unto you and ye shall be my sons and daughters, saith the Lord Almighty."

(2 Corinthians 6:18)

"For the Lord comforts His people and will have compassion on His afflicted ones ... I will not forget you! See, I have engraved you on the palms of my hands ... Those who hope in me will not be disappointed."

(Isaiah 49:13, 16, 23)

When I feel down and depressed I tend not to care much about myself. When I recognise this is happening I force myself to take more interest in what clothes I wear. I dress in brighter colours. I have a pamper time in the bath with special bubbles, lotions, potions and perfume. I force myself to eat when I'd rather not eat all day. I go for a walk, listen to some uplifting music, watch a comedy to make me laugh. We need to love and care for ourselves. It's important. If we don't, how can we expect someone else to care for us? After all, they're not God. He's the only One who loves us more than anyone else could.

4. Be sociable.

"A man that hath friends must show himself friendly; and there is a friend that sticketh closer than a brother."

(Proverbs 18:24)

Friendship is a special thing. I remember when I was young, my best friend and I would chat on the phone for hours, much to the amazement and shock of our families, who couldn't understand what we could possibly be talking about for so long! However, it meant a lot to us to have someone there through the ups and downs; someone we knew we could trust and confide in. Friendship goes both ways. We have to be a friend to have friends. Nurture and value your friendships. Spend time together, have fun, call each other, encourage each other, pray for your friends. You may find a friend to be closer than family, but remember that your family can be your friends too! Treasure the friends you have and be open to making connections with new people. Be sociable. Try out new activities, interests and hobbies; you never know who you may meet along the way. If necessary, force yourself to get out there more. It may be good preparation and practice for meeting your heart's desire.

5. Be hard working.

"Whatever your hand finds to do, do it with all your might."

(Ecclesiastes 9:10)

"All hard work brings a profit, but mere talk leads only to poverty."

(Proverbs 14:23)

It is good to find something productive and useful to do with our lives. A job or career can give purpose and help fulfil God's plan for us. We need to get to know ourselves and discover what skills, talents and abilities we have been given, ask for God's guidance in the work we pursue. Working hard with integrity is important. It's not just working hard when the boss is watching, but also when the boss is not there. The biblical truth applies, *"Do unto others as you would have them do to you."*

Remember the three R's? Rebecca, Rachel and Ruth.

Rebecca met the servant of her future father-in-law, Abraham, while going to get water at the well. She was kind enough to draw water for a stranger and his camels – which couldn't have been easy work. Have you seen the size of camels? They drink loads of water! But her kindness and hard work eventually led to her marrying Isaac (Genesis 24:45, 46, 67).

Rachel was a shepherdess for her father, Laban, and was looking after the sheep when she met Jacob, who loved her so much that he worked for her father for 14 years so that she could be his wife (Genesis 29:9).

Ruth worked hard in the fields to look after her mother-in-law, Naomi, even though she didn't have to. Since her husband was no longer alive, technically Naomi wasn't her mother-in-law any more. But through her care and hard work, Ruth earned the respect of the community and especially Boaz, the land owner, and she became his wife (Ruth 2:11-12).

Working hard at our daily tasks, caring for others, being hospitable to people, even strangers, can bring us into contact with people who are potential husbands or may, by association, lead us to them. Who knows what can happen through hard work.

6. Consider how to develop the best personal qualities.
Sometimes we hear people saying, "That's just how I am. Accept me for who I am." I think there is room for us all to develop into better people. We come to Christ as we are, but He wants to renew us, if we are willing to change for the better.

"Do not be conformed to this world (this age), [fashioned after and adapted to its external, superficial customs], but be

transformed (changed) by the [entire] renewal of your mind [by its new attitude], so that you may prove [for yourselves] what is the good and acceptable and perfect will of God, even the thing which is good and acceptable and perfect [in His sight for you]."

(Romans 12:2 AMP)

If we want to do God's will then we need to know how He expects us to behave. I checked out Proverbs for some wisdom on this from the wise man, Solomon. It is interesting that Solomon wasn't always wise about everything – especially when it came to excess. He knew a lot of women, having 700 wives and 300 concubines. Surely, that was not wise! But despite this, God taught him some noteworthy things:

- **Be a woman of noble character**. If we exhibit fine personal qualities and moral principles, this will be a blessing not only to us, but also to the community we live in, and to our husband.

"A wife of noble character who can find? She is worth far more than rubies. Her husband has full confidence in her and lacks nothing of value."

(Proverbs 31:10-11)

"He who finds a wife finds what is good and receives favour from the Lord."

(Proverbs 18:22, NIV)

- **Be prudent.**

"Houses and riches are an inheritance from fathers, but a

prudent wife is from the Lord."

(Proverbs 19:14, NKJV)

The word prudent means "wise in handling practical matters, exercising good judgment or common sense, careful about one's own interests and conduct." These are qualities we should possess.

• Be understanding, not contentious and angry.

"It is better to dwell in the wilderness than with a contentious and an angry woman."

(Proverbs 21:19)

Instead be understanding.

"He who is slow to anger has great understanding [and profits from his self-control]."

(Proverbs 14:29, AMP)

"Understanding is like a fountain of life to those who have it."

(Proverbs 16:22, NIRV)

• Self-control is essential.

"A person without self-control is like a city with broken–down walls."

(Proverbs 25:28, NLT)

- **Be careful and wise about what you say.**

"A wise man's heart guides his mouth, and his lips promote instruction. Pleasant words are a honeycomb, sweet to the soul and healing to the bones."

(Proverbs 16:23-24)

- **Love and life is not about having lots of stuff.**

"A simple life in the Fear of God is better than a rich life with a ton of headaches."

(Proverbs 15:16, MSG)

"It is better to eat soup with someone you love than steak with someone you hate."

(Proverbs 15:17, TLB)

- **Love is a doing word.** Love is...

"Patient, kind, does not envy, does not boast, is not proud, is not rude, is not self-seeking, is not easily angered, keeps no record of wrongs. Love does not delight in evil but rejoices with the truth. It always protects, always trusts, always hopes, and always perseveres. Love never fails."

(1 Corinthians 13: 4-8)

If we can strive to become more loving in character, like God, then we will become the kind of woman God wants us to be for our husbands. I believe He will also provide the husbands who will love us as He intends.

7. **Be cheerful.** Let's be happy we're alive! Isn't there so much to be thankful for? Life itself is such a blessing. Many, I am sure, would wish they could still be here. We have that gift, so let's enjoy life and live it to the full. We have a lot of good things to focus on that will give us a more cheerful spirit.

"A merry heart maketh a cheerful countenance."

(Proverbs 15:13)

"He that is of a merry heart hath a continual feast."

(Proverbs 15:15)

"A merry heart doeth good like a medicine, but a broken spirit drieth the bones."

(Proverbs 17:22)

"The spirit of a man will sustain his infirmity; but a wounded spirit who can bear?"

(Proverbs 18:14)

We stand a better prospect of getting through difficult circumstances with a cheerful spirit than a broken one. It's not easy, but let's try to "Look at the bright side of life." Think positive:

"Whatever is true, whatever is noble, whatever is right, whatever is pure, whatever is lovely, whatever is admirable, if anything is excellent or praiseworthy – think about such things."

(Philippians 4:8)

8. **Encourage yourself and others.** We use words every day to talk to ourselves (I'm not alone in doing this am I?) or to talk to others. We can use words that encourage and uplift or damage and destroy. Consider the words you use. Make a conscious effort to be more encouraging to yourself and those around you:

"A man has joy in giving an appropriate answer, and how good and delightful is a word spoken at the right moment – how good it is!"

(Proverbs 15:23, AMP)

Here are some encouraging verses to read:

God is with you (see Zephaniah 3:17-20)
Wait, have faith (see Habakkuk 2:3-4)
God cares (see Nahum 1:7)
God hears (see Jonah 2:2, 6-7)
God will restore (Joel 2:25-26)
You will live (Ezekiel 37:13-14)
God will rebuild (Ezekiel 36:35-36)

• **Trust God.** When we trust God to work things out for us, we can rest confidently, like a child in His arms, knowing that everything will eventually work out for our good. This will enable us to have peace of mind.

"You will keep him in perfect peace, whose mind is stayed on You; because he trusts in You. Trust in the Lord for ever, for in the Lord Jehovah is everlasting strength ... Yes, in the way of Your judgements, O Lord, we have waited for You; the desire of our soul is for Your name and for the remembrance of You."

(Isaiah 26:3-4, 8)

The desire of our soul is ultimately God, our Father. He is the only One who can really fill us up inside, heal our brokenness, and make us whole. We need to keep Him in mind throughout our journey as singles – or in whatever situation in life we find ourselves. We wait on Him and trust that when He sees fit, He is willing and able to change our situation. We need to trust His judgment on this matter. Marriage is too special a gift for us to choose for ourselves without God. Only God knows us and our heart. He is wise and qualified as our Father to be the best matchmaker.

As we move into the future, let us remain hopeful that God will provide for our needs. When we are afraid and worried, and those days will come, let us hold onto our Father and His Word.

"If you shall ask anything in my name, I will do it."

(John 10:14)

"Peace I leave with you. My peace I give unto you ... Let not your heart be troubled, neither let it be afraid."

(John 14:27)

Reflect:
Whatever may happen in your life, do not forget that your ultimate goal is to be reunited with your Heavenly Father. He loves you and as you journey towards your destination He will be with you to guide and provide for you.

Meditate:
"I do not consider myself yet to have taken hold of it. But one thing I do: Forgetting what is behind and straining towards what is ahead, I press on towards the goal to win the prize for

which God has called me heavenwards in Christ Jesus."

(Philippians 3:13-14)

"And my God will meet all your needs according to His glorious riches in Christ Jesus."

(Philippians 4:19)

"I am the Lord your God, who teaches you what is best for you, who directs you in the way you should go."

(Isaiah 48:17)

"The Lord your God is with you, He is mighty to save. He will take great delight in you, He will quiet you with His love, He will rejoice over you with singing ... 'I will give you honour and praise among all the peoples of the earth when I restore your fortunes before your very eyes,' says the Lord."

(Zephaniah 3:17, 20)

Pray:
Write a prayer to your Heavenly Father and tell Him how you feel. Ask for the love and guidance you need for each day:

Printed in Poland
by Amazon Fulfillment
Poland Sp. z o.o., Wrocław